WAYFINDING

A MEMOIR

WAYFINDING
A Memoir
By Renee Gilmore

Copyright © October 1, 2025 Renee Gilmore

No part of this book may be used or performed without written consent of the author, if living, except for critical articles or reviews.

Gilmore, Renee
1st edition

ISBN: 978-1-949487-62-6
Library of Congress Control Number: 2025930906

Interior design by Patrick Werle
Cover design by Baonhia Xiong
Cover Art by Maya Kuvaja
Editing by Richard Terrill

Trio House Press, Inc.
Minneapolis, MN
www.triohousepress.org

To my husband Steven who helped light the way.

Table of Contents

INTRODUCTION

Mapping   5

DESTINATION UNKNOWN

Another Woman's Name   11

DRIFT

The Closet*   25

COORDINATES

Colvill Park 1976   33

BACK BEARING

The Longest Ride*   43

It's Called the Lingual Frenulum*   56

POSTCARDS FROM THE ROAD: PART I

I-40^   81

A Bible Story^   83

FIX

Getaway Car   93

EPHEMERALS

The Rites of Spring   101

The Ambulance   112

Malibu   126

The Shrilling   136

CARDINAL POSITION

Migration: El Paso 1999   145

The Brown Jug   161

When I Was a Ghost   178

The Kidnapper   188

RANGE LIGHTS

Haleakala Blues   201

Dayton is Not an Uber Town   209

TRANSIT

Whippin' Shitties   215

Driving Lessons   221

The Monaco Grand Prix (As One Does)   234

AS THE CROW FLIES

The Garage   249

Why is Tom in The Trunk?	266
Dancing With The Gravedigger	271
Jonni Lynn	286

POSTCARDS FROM THE ROAD: PART II

Angels in Plaid Shirts	299
Sing Your Hymn of the Open Road	305
Leaving Is What We Do	309
Apologies to My Body	321

TRUE NORTH

Waffle House Redemption	315
The Grief Competition: My Name Was ____	325

Acknowledgments	331
Previously Published Work	335
About the Author	337

Content Warnings:
*CW: Sexual Abuse/Assault
^CW: Domestic Violence

Mapping

Okay, let's start with a spoiler alert: I am still alive, still here. There are myriad reasons why this should not be the case. But this is not to say that I'm unscathed, unbroken, and that I haven't lost precious things along the way. PTSD, trauma, and grief have done an admirable job of changing my neurobiology around memory, for one thing. Which is a fancy way to say I can't remember shit. And, because I'm not young, I can't remember shit anyway. I can't remember the name of the hotel in Monaco, the last time I had my car serviced, or where I left my phone half the time. But what I can remember, do remember, in deep, technicolor, visceral detail are the traumatic events in my life. If you have experienced trauma, you know exactly what I mean. The extreme sharpness with which I remember details is almost physically painful. I often think, how miraculous would it be if I could file down the edges of those memories, blur the details, and extricate the sensations that are memory-bound in my skin. Dull the smells, decades-old that put me on high alert. Release the fear that pounces when I hear footfalls behind me. Life without those things would be glorious, but for now, that is just a fantasy. For now, there is other work to be done. There is the job of remembering.

It has been devastatingly difficult work to agitate and awaken the memories that have been dormant all these years. To try to make sense of myself, reconcile what happened to me, and sort through reasons for critical, and often terrible decisions I made that set me up for lifelong heartache. This work is further complicated by the fact that I learned in my thirties that I am not even who I thought I was. My name is not the one I was given by my mother at birth; that name was stolen by my father. There is a lot to unpack, and I try not to feel constantly angry and wounded.

    I'm endlessly mining, burrowing and sorting like a furred animal in the earth. I dig, but here is a secret: I feel like a truth-seeking imposter, a phony. Because I simply don't want to remember; it's too damn hard most days. But I must remember, to heal, and therein lies the tension. I show my mask of a mask of a smile and say I'm okay, but I feel neither admirable nor brave. There is a certain element of misery in the unpacking, the unburdening.

    I've been thinking about why I've felt compelled to recall, examine, and contextualize so many events in my life. It came down to this: I was exhausted from dragging the weight of the chains of my past behind me. The secrets. The lies that were told. I've been moving ahead and getting ahead, sure. But I have internalized enormous shame and hardcoded my secrets. I also somehow concluded that joy was a privilege, not a right, at least for me. In some of my greatest times of happiness, the birth of my son, marrying my husband, and getting my advanced degree, I reflexively imposed restrictions on my joy and throttled my exhilaration. I felt in my heart I was undeserving of good, of pleasure.

    In my process of recollection, I summoned the dead,

the long discarded, and I coerced them to whisper our shared stories. To pull me back to those times, those places. To make me feel. Through this process of remembering again and again, the memories eventually took shape, like cells stitching together into an organ.

I've written this book as honestly and accurately as I could. But, due to the passage of time and the impact of trauma, some of my memories have degraded like a copy of a copy of a copy. It's exhausting and sad.

With this sometimes-unreliable memory, I understood the importance of fact-checking. I heavily relied on fact-checkers and fact-checking tools. My brother Tim was invaluable in helping me with dates, people, details, timelines, and other minutiae. My husband Steven was helpful, too, as were my son, Samson, and other family members and friends. I relied on multiple beta readers, editors, my therapist, the library, and the internet to confirm facts, including the geographies I describe, and the contextual details of the eras I reference. I also sorted through more than 750 family photos, seeking triggers and recollections.

Any errors in this book are completely mine. I have slightly changed some names, details, places, and events because not every story is mine to tell. You'll read about awful things that happened to me. Some stories may be upsetting or triggering to some readers. These stories upset me, too, but they need to be told.

Which brings us back to the fact that I am still here. I'm

happier. I'm healthier. I think of myself in the context of a diamond. Somehow, with my life's burdens and pressures, I turned the inky carbon of grief, sorrow, and fear into a reasonable facsimile of a diamond. Somewhat shiny, yet imperfect to the eye. I don't think there is enough cutting, grinding, and shaping to ever turn me into what I would ever consider good enough.

The engagement ring Steve gave me is brilliant and beautiful, with a tiny, black dot of carbon that you can see if you look hard enough. The only way to get imperfections out of a diamond is to drill them out and fill the holes with a molten lead glass-like substance. This book has pushed me to do that, and I feel the pain of those extractions. But I can celebrate and enjoy the beauty that comes after. There is far more life behind me than in front of me, and I intend to grab all the joy I can.

DESTINATION UNKNOWN

Another Woman's Name

In 1965, my parents, Michael and Margaret, working-class devotees of the American Dream™, bought their first house in Fremont, California. They had been married just two years, saving as much money as they could, and imagining what it would be like to have a house of their own. They would fill it with love, with children, and the trappings of modern consumerism.

Similar to my parents' new marriage, Fremont had been recently incorporated. Rows and rows of tract houses were planted as a new cash crop, fulfilling the American dream of homeownership for many working-class families. Fremont, today a part of Silicon Valley, is unrecognizable as that boom town of the 1960s, brimming with promise. But, optimism remains, as it's now an enclave for newly minted tech bros who can afford what are now multi-million-dollar bungalows.

In 1965, in every direction from where the model home office had staked its flag, single-family, single-story, tan and beige homes with brown roofs popped out of the ground like stucco mushrooms. The little house my parents were desperate to own had a nearly unattainable price tag of $26,000. They were determined to do whatever it took to buy it. Both of them worked, and worked hard. My father in a muffler shop in Hayward, and my mother in the secretarial pool at Shell Oil in Menlo Park. That summer of

1965, after borrowing cash from every friend and relative they could think of, they closed on the new house, which still needed some finishing work. They did not shy away from building sweat equity. They never shied away from work.

The house closing was not without drama. The week before the closing date, my parents had panicked. They found out they were pregnant with me, their first child. In those days, if a woman was pregnant, none of her wages counted as income for the mortgage qualification. They were terrified that somehow the mortgage company would find out. My mother told me that after they successfully finished the closing and were leaving the building with the house keys, she stepped off the sidewalk in her high heels and nylons, and threw up in the bushes. From the stress or morning sickness, my mother said she barfed like a pro.

Once my parents moved into the house, the pressure of the closing was replaced with the pressure to finish the house before I arrived. My father was very handy, and he did much of the carpentry and painting himself. He worked six days a week at the muffler shop and spent evenings and Sundays finishing doors, laying sod, planting trees, and putting in bushes. My mother, who had dreamed of being a fashion designer, was an excellent seamstress. She spent her evenings cutting, pinning, and sewing window curtains out of faded floral bedsheets and pillowcases, her loud, brown Singer sewing machine clacking into the night. In the first couple of years, they ate lots of eggs and toast, hot dogs and beans, and tuna sandwiches.

****

I never knew my father was a thief. He confessed to me, in astonishing detail and without remorse, the night of my mother's funeral. It was 2001, and I was 34 years old.

I was born at Stanford University Hospital on the Tuesday of Holy Week. It was 1966, and Star Trek had just debuted on TV, Lyndon Johnson was president, and daily protests against the war in Vietnam were splashed on the evening news in low contrast black and white. The outside world was chaotic. But, my parents, Michael and Margaret, tried to create a domestic oasis inside their small house. Each evening, after my mother cleared the dinner table and the leftovers were tucked into Tupperware, she and my father stepped down into the sunken living room, with its dark green shag carpet, and arranged themselves on the couch. They waited for Bonanza, The Beverly Hillbillies, or The Virginian to come on. Hunkered together, the commotion of the rest of the world felt far away. My mother rested her hands on her rounded belly, full of a baby and poorly camouflaged under a tent of a floral housedress. She didn't know if I would be a boy or a girl, but she had dreamed of a red-headed daughter filling the house with giggles and dancing.

She just knew that a girl would transform her life. And, my mother may have been unsure about many things, but when it came to naming her baby girl, she knew, without question, what to do.

Going back generations, members of my mother's side of the family were mostly impoverished tenant farmers, both in County Wexford in Ireland and later, in America, with very little in the way of physical things that didn't serve a practical purpose. There were artifacts of hard-boiled peasant Catholicism: A Bible, a cross, a rosary, and in later years, a painting of The Last Supper. During the Potato Famine, before my great-grandmother came to America with only one shoe, it was more important to eat than to collect pretty things.

In my family, the men implemented law and order; the women ran a secret matriarchy. The women ruled the gardens and kitchens. They could not do much about the poverty, the beatings, the drinking, the neglect. But there was more than one well-timed whisper in the confessional, to prompt a visit by the parish priest.

The women in my family were also the documentarians, the keepers of memories. The men were busy in the fields. They were concerned with rain, hail, and paying for seed. They fixed broken machinery. They tended to sick calves and lame horses. They had no time for women's things: recipes, babies, first communions, sick children, recording events in the family Bible. The men may have been storytellers, but the women archived the truth.

In my mother's family, the reigning matriarch was the caretaker of that family Bible. It was our Catholic library, to be consulted in times of joy and despair during Lent and the Resurrection. The matriarch was the trusted custodian, until death or the ravages of dementia, which seized the last three matriarchs before my mother, and rendered them unable to fulfill their critical duty. Then the next in line solemnly received her small inheritance: the Bible with the worn brown cover and tissue pages, filled with birthdates and deaths, marriages and baptisms; a blue fountain pen ca.1899; some tortoiseshell hair clips; and a few sepia-toned photos. There was no generational wealth, no jewelry, artwork, or collections of any kind to be valued, or fought over. The only jewels passed down in my family for at least five generations, from the women to the girls, were names. The names: Mary, Margaret, Elizabeth, Eleanor, Lillian.

    Weeks before I was born, my parents discussed baby names. My father was firm. A boy would be named Michael, after him. My mother was firm. A girl would be named ___. There was no more discussion.

    When my mother's contracting body failed to pump me into the cool world, anesthesia was dripped into her veins, and like slicing an oyster and removing the pearl, gloved hands lifted me from her body. When she woke, bleary, disoriented, a nurse presented me to her, a pink and white swaddle, full of promise and squall. My mother pulled me close for the first time, and in that space between commotion and calm in her hospital room, she called me _____, without hesitation. It was the first gift she gave me, one of few she could offer. My mother blessed me with my name and between waking and dozing in her hospital bed, in quiet rituals that only she and I shared, she told me about the names. About the women. Mary, Margaret, Elizabeth, Eleanor, Lillian, and the rest.

When I was three days old, my father stole my name.

It was Good Friday, and my father left my mother as she dozed in her hospital bed, no longer tethered by the tubes and wires feeding the machines that told her body's secrets. My father headed for the elevator, the one that would take him to the main floor of the hospital. He had an important mission, and it had everything to do with me.

The elevator brought my father to the first floor of the hospital. He looked at the signs on the wall and chose his direction. He strode with purpose, flat top haircut, mutton-chop sideburns. His black, or maybe brown, zip-up leather Chelsea boots squeaked on linoleum floors, freshly waxed. Coins jingled in his pockets, the nickels and quarters synchronizing with the flat-toned overhead pages and the clattering metal carts passing him in the corridor. The soundtrack of change. A symphony of disharmony. He found what he was looking for: the door to the hospital records office.

My father greeted the cute (according to him) young woman behind the counter. He had a singular task. He asked for the forms and a pen. He filled them out, in his best handwriting, bold block letters. He signed his name. His signature looked like a heartbeat, the pointed tops of M, and L, high above the choppy squiggle of the rest of the letters. In less than ten minutes, it was done. Like a bandit, he stole my name, my identity, and my birthright, just by signing his name with a flourish. His name held greater currency than mine ever could. My mother slept, unaware in her room, and I slept, unaware, snug in my bassinet in the nursery, my pink name card affixed over my head. As my father left the records office, he heard the chik-chik, chik-chik of typewriter keys behind him, the thwack of metal letters hitting the form. His task was completed, and he was pleased with himself. Maybe he whistled as he returned to my mother's room. I often wonder if he understood that sometimes what is done, can never be undone. I wonder if he cared.

    My father erased the name given to me, gifted to me, and replaced it with the name of a stranger. He chose Renee. Why? Was she an old (or not so old) girlfriend? Likely. Maybe she was the waitress, the secretary, the stewardess. Those are the women I know about. Maybe she was the woman in the photo I found in the very back of his desk drawer. Dark brown hair piled on top of her head, a lacquer of hairspray cementing the confection in place. Siren red lipstick, green eyes, tight blue sweater interrupted by large, pointy breasts. How long did my father ruminate on my name? How many choices did he have? I imagine their smiling faces and make up their names: Evelyn, Renee, Patricia, Susan, Denise, Linda, Joyce, Delores, Rita.

    When my father filled out the form, he also claimed my middle name and changed it from ___ to Michelle, the most feminine version of his name he could think of. Could this have been his way of acknowledging me? Or just him getting his way, in his role as the male head of the household in the 1960s? Maybe all of these things. Maybe none of them.

Just like that, it was done. My identity was stolen. I was left with this other woman's name. It was as if my name, the person I was for those three days, had never existed. I imagine how my mother whispered my name as she held me, her mouth close to my tiny pink ear. For three days, she said my name like a prayer of gratitude and wonder, to summon my ancestors: Mary, Elizabeth, Margaret, Eleanor, Lillian, all the others - those past generations of tough, independent, and imperfect women, asking them to keep me safe and make me strong. To her, mustering these women was like calling God.

The ritual, the gift, the blessing of my name had held no value to my father. After those moments in the registration office, form, pen, signature, and typewriter, I was alive, but my name was dead.

My father did not tell my mother what he had done.

My mother found out three days later when she and I were finally discharged from the hospital. My father pushed the handles of the metal wheelchair toward the lobby doors, while my mother cradled me tightly in her arms. My father couldn't juggle the discharge paperwork and push the wheelchair, so he handed the folder to my mother. She opened it. She saw my tiny footprints, inked on white paper. My black and white birth photo. Then she saw a white carbon copy of the form with my new name. She was stunned. My mother felt the wall of loss and wailed. She tearfully berated my father, right there in the lobby. My father was embarrassed. He was shy and hated being the center of attention. And he did not appreciate being publicly castigated by his wife. He told my mother she was being too emotional. To stop causing a scene. I wonder if he said, *you're scaring the baby*?

My father parked the wheelchair in front of the hospital, left us, and brought the car around. He helped my mother out of the wheelchair and maneuvered her into the passenger seat. Once settled, she positioned me against her chest. My father put my mother's small blue vinyl suitcase in the back seat and prepared himself for the ride home. This was my first car ride. It was not what either of my parents had expected.

In those days, car seats for newborns were not widely available, and my parents didn't own one. During that ride home, my mother hugged me tightly all the way home from the hospital – a very long 45 minutes across the Bay Area. Because she had a C-section, her lap seat belt hung limply off the side of the seat, discarded. She clutched me, gritted her teeth, and stared forward. The minutes and miles ticked by. She refused to say one word to my father, despite his prodding, his attempts to be funny. He joked about me being an Easter baby, and that he could tell people I was delivered by the Easter Bunny, in an Easter basket, instead of by the stork. When she didn't respond, his irritation grew.

My father told me, that night of my mother's funeral, that he had dreamed about that car ride for months, and pictured what it was going to be like. He, a proud papa behind the wheel, bringing his son, his boy, home from the hospital. (It never occurred to him that he may get a daughter instead.) He had spent hours washing the car, carefully drying it with the damp tan chamois that squeaked when he pulled it across the hood. He waxed the car, methodically wiping on the thick paste with one of his old white t-shirts, which were kept in a stack in the garage. He cleaned out the ashtrays and vacuumed the seats and floors. He wanted everything to be perfect. But that car ride that should have been full of excitement and wonderment, was tense, unpleasant. Between the deep anxiety around getting us home safely and my mother's palpable seething, it was not the joyful journey anyone had planned. While my father was telling me everything, that night of the funeral, he didn't seem particularly remorseful or emotional. He was matter-of-fact about all of it.

My baby album has several photos of my mother holding me the day they brought me home. She is squinting in the sun, smiling, or at least showing her teeth, in front of our little tan stucco, one-story house. She was wearing a sleeveless dress that concealed her shape, the bulges and swelling from carrying me and her uterine support system not yet deflated. I'm tightly swaddled in layers of crocheted baby blankets, pink, blue, and yellow. In those photos, the car that got us home is nearly out of frame. The images look like an advertisement for The Good Life™ in the California suburbs in the 1960s: Wife, car, house, lawn, baby. My father must have taken the photos. He is absent in every image.

I'm angry with my father. I wonder who I could have been if he had selected a different name from the women he knew. Would I have been happier, more successful, less damaged by the life I lived? But more importantly, who would I have become if he hadn't changed my name in the first place? In some ways, I feel like the girl with my original name is my twin who died outside the womb. She never became who she was meant to be.

Since that night of my mother's funeral, I have thought about her, the other me, the potential me, often, and mourned her. I'm not ready to let her go. Though I don't regularly attend Mass any longer, I light a candle and say a small prayer for her when I find myself at a Catholic church. Rest in peace, Amy Elizabeth. Rest in peace.

DRIFT

The Closet

It was just after lunch on a hot Minnesota August day. The air felt less like air and more like a viscous coating. Even the cicadas had paused their whine. The hours stretched before me until the house came alive again. The chattering of my little brother as he stumbled around the grownups as toddlers do. The clinking of glasses with cheap before-dinner Cutty Sark scotch and water and ice, followed by the after-dinner Cutty Sark scotch. No water. No ice. Sometimes right from the bottle, if no one was looking. There were not yet cooking smells, no baking of lemon cake pie or the biscuits my grandmother seemed to conjure up from nearly nothing.

That summer, those hours and hours and hours between breakfast and safety had become the time of the ritual. Maybe sacred, maybe grotesque. I told myself: Pay close attention. Listen. Strain to hear his green truck, slightly rusted around the gills. The truck I rode in the previous summer in Colorado to go fishing for perch with him. When I was the only one he invited. When I pressed my knees against my door the whole way. The truck with the muffler like the low growl of an angry bear. Now: Listen for it slowing as it turns in the driveway. Listen for the engine to rev one final time, then the engine ticking, then silence. Listen for the truck door to slam. Listen and count. Listen and prepare. Be ready. Be smart. Be brave.

The back door opened with a turning of the doorknob, an achy squeak, and closed with a soft whoomp, as the pressure in the house changed. The turning and click of the lock sounded final. Like the end of a story. Like the delineation between before and after. Like a jailer just doing his job. Listen. I held on to a tiny sliver of hope. But, there was no leathery thump of my mother's purse dropping on the kitchen table, or the papery sound of People magazine and bills skittering across the counter. No jingling of pocket change or the metallic landing of my father's keys on the hook next to the phone on the wall.

It was him. I knew what was next. I was in my bedroom with the pink wallpaper, the polka dot curtains, the stuffed animals. I knew what to do.

First, ignore the pounding heart, the tickles of bile in the back of my throat, the tiny tears forming (panic, pity, resignation?). Close my book, quietly – Laura Ingalls Wilder and the Big Woods would have to wait. Get up and quickly, quietly, like a ninja in my Minnie Mouse t-shirt, push the bedroom door closed, with a swoosh of an arc across the carpet, and click it closed. The door had no lock.

Next, drop to hands and knees, quickly, quietly, go around the bed, and crawl past the white built-in bookcase. Open the wooden closet door, quickly, quietly, and scoot into the dusty darkness. Pull the door closed behind me, but not too hard – the wood cannot rattle. A gentle click. Scuttle backward, like a hermit crab, and part the dresses and waves of dry-cleaning bags. Let them flow before me like a curtain. Wait and listen. Wait for the size 13 boots – creaks in the hallway.

The bedroom door whispers open across the carpet, and closes slowly, with a click. He whistles tunelessly – this is his favorite game, apex predator versus little girl prey. I feel the energy of his determination as he searches. I hear the effort of him lifting the dust ruffle and the grunt as he checks under the bed. His arthritic knees crack with the bending. The whistling stops - he is getting frustrated. I changed my hiding place.

He comes around the bed, past the white built-in bookshelves, and stops just outside the brown wooden door of the closet. He puts his hand on the worn gold knob and turns it slowly. Like the moment is so delicious he is pausing to savor it. He swings the door open and the afternoon light pours into the tiny square space. Dust motes twirl with the movement and make their hasty escape.

I wedge myself into the back corner, tucking my knees under my chin, quickly, and quietly. Becoming smaller and smaller yet. Wishing myself out of existence.

Huge, old man, weather-roughened hands reach into the closet and part the sea of dresses and bags. He is smiling. And then he isn't. He exhales into the space– his breath sour with pipe tobacco and Listerine. His mitt-like hands cover the knobs of my knees, like a pot holder over an egg. They tighten and pull as the old hardwood floorboards scrape the bottom of my shorts. I try to stay upright and not hit my head. He releases my knees, (bony, scabbed) and encircles my ankles with those scarred hands, and drags me from safety. He's angry I made him work so hard. I wished I was older and stronger. I wished he would die. That I would die. Anything to make it stop.

He lifts me, roughly, like a bag of dog food, and drops me on the *bed. Pink shorts, smiley face underpants tugged quickly, quietly. I stare at the ceiling or maybe I close my eyes. I'm there, but I'm not. I'm too numb to feel scared or angry. It ends with a whoosh or a click or silence. He whistles or he doesn't, he says things or he doesn't, time stretches and suspends. None of these things mattered anymore, and I couldn't tell or remember the difference. In my head the mantra, the prayer, the pleading: Just please don't kill my little brother. I had heard this threat from him so many times it was infused in my muscles and bones.*

Sometimes when I recall those times, I swear I can hear him breathing, I can feel his callused hands on my body. When I was in high school, he got lung cancer and was on life support for six weeks. Then my grandfather, that horrible grandfather, John, died. I pretended I was sad. The funeral was in Colorado, and I didn't have to go. Years later, I visited the cemetery and spit on his grave. I felt embarrassed and exposed, but I was not sorry.

My body remembers far more than my brain does. When I was pregnant with my son, every time I smelled Listerine, I threw up, once in the Kmart parking lot. It was the same with pipe tobacco and Right Guard deodorant. I learned about sensory triggers the hard way. I dated a very nice guy in college, and I made him switch his deodorant to a different brand. I didn't tell him why, and I could tell he thought I was weird.

After a couple of false starts, I began therapy when my son was five, the age at which I first remember the abuse starting. I had to. I felt crazy. After a few sessions, the therapist was able to pry off a tiny bit of my decades-thick armor. I cried for the entire sessions and nearly hyperventilated. When I talked about him in therapy, I felt his hands around my ankles. His hands roaming my little girl body. It took several years to shift the blame from myself, from my perceived failure to protect myself, to him, where it belonged.

Eventually, when I talked about him, about what he did to me I was able to move from feelings of suffocating dread and terror, into anger. Into rage, really. Messy, sometimes misplaced fury. He stole my childhood, my happiness, my joy. The trauma he inflicted fractured my soul, and I lost my ability to trust. Or, I chose to trust the wrong people, with disastrous results. He marked me, he made me vulnerable to other predators. I suffered because of him.

The trauma he wreaked on me impacted my memory. For years I struggled to retain and recall information, events, and even mundane things. I was nearly incapable of memorizing. Even now I'll look at a photo from my childhood and often have no recollection of what I'm looking at. That makes me angry, but most of all it makes me sad.

In adulthood, I was finally diagnosed with a disability that impacts my ability to process numbers and spatial relationships, and recall information. Who knows if my lifelong trauma, starting with what he did changed my neurobiology. I have to think so.

The earliest time I remember the abuse, I was five years old, and wearing a yellow dress. It may have started earlier, like it did for my two female cousins and also my aunt. She and I talked about it once, and she couldn't say anything more about it and insisted she was fine. I am still not fine. But I'm getting better.

COORDINATES

Colvill Park, 1976

We waited in the cool early June morning in my small Minnesota town. The weather was just beginning to nudge toward a hot and humid summer. It was the summer of freedom. Our parents had signed us up for these swimming lessons weeks before, to keep us from drowning in the Mississippi and to keep us from asking *what's there to do* fifty times a day. Now we knew the routine. We gathered on the sidewalk outside the hulking concrete and brick pool building, yawning, all bony arms and legs, shag haircuts, and red, white, and blue t-shirts, flagging the bicentennial. The pool building was just yards from the river, and we could watch the barges and tugboats trudging up and down the channel.

We changed quickly in the locker rooms, our toes starting to prune on the cold, wet, textured concrete floor. I tried to ignore the girl bodies around me, naked and awkward, as I ducked my head and maneuvered under my towel, embarrassed and nervous to display my body. My heart quickened and my mouth dried. I constantly felt the sensation of someone watching me. I was hypervigilant, always. That morning was around the time I started separating from my body. Started to actively hate it. Started becoming interested in dieting and making my body smaller, less visible. That was maybe a way I could survive.

Swimsuits were problematic for me in so many ways.

The summer before, or maybe it was earlier that year, my mother and I were shopping for swimsuits at the little department store on Main Street when the sky went deep green, then black. I was standing alone in a dressing room in my underwear when the store manager yelled for everyone to get to the basement. The tornado sirens were howling. The huge plate glass windows facing the street were starting to slightly throb from the pressure change. My mother screamed at me to hurry up, grab my clothes, run, and get dressed downstairs. But the idea of the store employees and customers seeing me in my underpants was more than I could stand. It felt worse than whatever the tornado was going to do. I put on my clothes as fast as I could and flew out of the dressing room. My mother and I scrambled down the wide stairs to the basement and took shelter along with everyone else from the store under big white tables covered with dozens and dozens of colorful bolts of fabric. That tornado popped those plate glass windows and we heard them explode, one after another. Some people say a tornado sounds like a train, but I think it sounds like a meat grinder hungrily chewing up everything in its path. The tornado blasted down Main Street, along the Mississippi, eventually traveling to our house, miles west of downtown. The tornado stripped leaves from our trees and peeled off much of the roof on our porch and garage, while my father, completely oblivious, worked downstairs in his woodshop, table saw running at full volume. Once the tornado passed, my mother and I carefully picked our way through the glass-dappled store, got to our car, and drove home. When we got there, my father was still in the basement, and my brother, a toddler was taking a nap in his bedroom next to the porch. It appeared he didn't even wake up during the tornado. I remember my mother, unhinged, unloading on my father for nearly getting their son killed. I don't remember anyone asking me how I was doing.

On that June Tuesday morning, I was wearing my purple swimsuit with the bottom that always sagged on my skinny behind, and I was ready to swim. Or at least ready to get it over with. Whistles blew and lessons commenced. Our small army of almost-swimmers was ordered into the blue sea of the outdoor pool – Olympic-sized, unheated, the only one in town. We had already learned that easing into the water was the worst idea. We jumped in and clung to the rough sides of the pool, dozens of us treading water like shipwrecked sailors hoping for a miracle.

We were a competitive pack. American crawl, sidestroke, and butterfly were our currency. We were all striving to earn another Red Cross card by learning a new skill, practicing, and getting promoted to the next group by the end of the summer. Minnow to Fish. Fish to Flying Fish. Flying Fish to Shark. Or maybe it was just beginning, intermediate, or advanced. We followed a parallel path to the swimmers at the YMCA in town, with its indoor heated pool. In later years, I swam there too. Year by year, level by level, we progressed from wailing and tears to flailing in the water, to controlling our limbs and gliding with confidence. The holy grail was permission to fly off the highest diving board, more than 20 feet above the water. Arms and legs akimbo, or tightened like a human arrow, or curled into a cannonball, clutching our knees, it was a rite of passage and completely terrifying. It's a miracle no one died. The actual divers, the teenagers, and the lifeguards, though, we worshipped like gods. We watched them practice, our eyes big, mouths slack, while we motored our feet furiously, clutching our kickboards. Later that summer, I got to dive off the low board, and I was thrilled. But the summer I was thirteen, the last year of Colvill Park swimming lessons, I got my chance to take on the high board.

I remember making my way up the narrow steps, each wet and coated with sandy grit. I remember grabbing the silver metal bars at the top, and slowly inching toward the end of the board. It was my brass ring, my Valhalla, my one shot. I felt the other swimmers watching me intently. There would be no practice round. I stood near the end of the board, psyching myself up. At the last second, I chickened out on the dive and decided to just cannonball in. Unfortunately, I leaned too far back and hit the water with a flat smack. The air wooshed out of my lungs as my back felt like I had shattered it. I sunk deeper into the water. Luckily, I was able to get my bearings and somewhat frantically flap my arms like a windmill and make my way to the surface before a lifeguard, if they were watching, felt the need to jump in and save me. I slowly scissor-kicked my way to the side of the pool and rested my head on the concrete. I did it. I went off the high board. But I felt no sense of triumph. Only shame and the ache of failure. All I could focus on was that I chickened out on the dive. That was the only time I remember going off the high board that summer, or ever.

That fall, I was in seventh grade, and I joined the swim team. After several practices at the big junior high pool, I learned I was not very good. I was also bullied by some of the other girls, especially Mary Jo. She was my chief tormentor, but she had her henchgirls too. One afternoon, when we were practicing for our second or maybe third competition, I hopped on the white starting block, at the shallow end, as I had done dozens of other times. I perched, tensed, and waited for the whistle. Kim, the top henchgirl, lurched at me from behind and shoved me forward. The momentum drove me straight to the blue bottom of the pool, where my forehead smacked the unyielding concrete.

I must have hit hard enough to lose consciousness because the next thing I remember I was floating in the water and our coach, Mr. Featherstone, was blowing his whistle furiously and running. The next thing I remember after that was seeing Kim, Mary Jo, and the other girls giggling uncontrollably. After that "accident," I took over as the stats manager and ran the clipboard for the rest of the season. I never dove into the water again.

At Colvill Park that morning, after our lesson, we made our way back to the locker room. I sat on the metal bench, under my tent of soggy towel, peeled off my swimsuit, and systematically reclothed myself. Once that summer, an older girl named Tina yanked off my towel and threw it on the puddled concrete. As I scrambled to cover my nakedness, she stood over me and laughed. When I started to cry, she pointed at me and laughed even louder. I don't know which was worse, the humiliation or the terror this violation invoked. I didn't understand at the time, but I was adding this trauma to my growing list.

Once we were dressed, wet swimsuits smooshed into plastic bags or rolled up into our towels, stringy hair poking our eyes, we stampeded the snack bar with coins jingling in our hands.

We sat at worn wooden picnic tables or on the matted grass, or walked around the park, slurping our Popsicles, and prying Tangy Taffy from our molars. Tired and satiated, we moved to the curb in front of the pool building, and waited for the parade of sedans, station wagons, and pickup trucks to arrive. Some parents were eager to hear about the morning's lesson, and others hurried and calculated the minutes until they had to be back at work. Every kid was picked up, and the vehicles pulled out on Highway 61, in an untidy, unplanned caravan. Every kid but me.

More often than not, I sat on the curb after the caravan departed and the street and the park returned to birdsong. I sat alone. I stretched and listened for my mother rounding the corner to the pool house, my hope rising each time a car drove up. I strained until all I could hear was the buzzing in my ears. I waited until I couldn't stand it any longer, until my anxiety skittered across my skin like an insect. I got up and shuffled into the dark pool building. Without making eye contact, I asked the teenager behind the metal counter if I could use the phone. I felt so ashamed. I had them dial my house phone number. I let it ring eight times and prayed someone would answer. Then I tried my grandparent's phone number, the good grandparents, the kind ones, Carl and Eleanor, who lived a mile away from us. As a last resort, I had them call my father's work, on the off-chance he was there. Eventually, as I sat stinking with chlorine and sadness, someone would arrive and drive me home.

 While the other kids were horsing around with their siblings and orchestrating complicated sleepovers with their friends like they were military maneuvers, I was in my room, alone. I heard the neighborhood kids playing Marco Polo and kick the can until the streetlights came on, the signal that the day had ended and it was time for bed. I lay in my bed in the dark, holding my stuffed Holly Hobby doll with one arm. Listening. Waiting. Planning. Calculating. I had become skilled in the art and science of survival.

BACK BEARING

A bearing that is the exact opposite of your destination or waypoint.

The Longest Ride

I was the first person in my family to go to college. There was no one to advise me, and I had no idea what I was doing. But I was determined. My parents, especially my father, were extremely and vocally disappointed that I was not staying in our small town to take over the family business. Somehow I had become a turncoat, and if not for my grandmothers, who each gave me some of their tiny savings, I wouldn't have been able to even think about attending college. I saved everything I could from my job at the Red Owl grocery store, and Liberty's restaurant. I was getting scholarships and student loans, and I was pretty sure I could squeak by.

I filled out the forms, mailed the applications, and created a magical place in my mind called COLLEGE™. I would have lots of friends, maybe even be popular. I would hang out with my girlfriends on the weekends, eat popcorn and pizza, and listen to music, only interrupted when my adorable boyfriend came by to say hello. The other girls would be so jealous. My grades would be great, even in math, which had always been problematic, due to an undiagnosed learning disability. I would get even more scholarships. It was going to be amazing. I was going to be amazing.

To make COLLEGE™ awesome, I knew, deep down, that I simply had to become someone else. In effect, create a new and improved persona, a new and improved me. I didn't know exactly how to go about this, but I obsessively, and maybe desperately believed it was the only way my future could be better than my past. This was my big chance to move four hours away, where nobody knew me—an opportunity to start over. I started making my list of what to change, which I hid under an encyclopedia in my bookcase.

1. New haircut (Reference: TEEN magazine and PEOPLE magazine)

2. New clothes (Preppy, cute)

3. Practice introducing my new self in front of the mirror (Smile bigger, sound friendly, smart, not weird)

4. Figure out how to go about getting a nice boyfriend (No sex)

That last one, sex, was my hold-back, my code—one thing I was saving for myself. I was waiting for that elusive, magical nice boyfriend, to be in an actual relationship, to have official sex. I had decided that nothing that happened to me in my childhood counted. The 18-year-old me deserved something better. I was taking small steps toward reclaiming my body, and my agency, giving myself the power and permission to say no and mean it. And it would work.

I was determined to succeed in all things COLLEGE™, especially the boyfriend part. The only boys and men interested in me in high school were not nice, and not boyfriend material. Especially the ginger-haired 23-year-old named Dan who I dated when I was not quite 17. He worked on a horse farm and wore dentures after a horse kicked out all his front teeth. Kissing someone with fake teeth is strange, but I didn't know any better at that time. Dan's brand of "affection," especially after a few beers or shots of Jack Daniels, was roughly grabbing me and repeatedly slapping my face, especially that time I had embarrassed him by telling his friends how young I was. They had yelled "jailbait!" over and over. Yet, Dan insisted that he wanted to take me to my junior prom and was willing to rent a baby blue tux with a white ruffle. My parents liked Dan, or at least they said they did, and I hid the purple shadows from his fingers on my arms. Against the advice of my friends, who thought he was great, I broke up with him. I didn't go to the junior prom and I gave away my long, lacy pink dress. The bruises from Dan's chunky high school class ring smacking my ribs eventually faded.

  I attempted, really tried to get a boyfriend my senior year. I failed. However, I did make out several times with the beautiful Brazilian exchange student named Luis, with his soulful brown eyes, and gentle manner. Every time he spoke to me, I felt tingly and maybe even a little more happy than scared. Unfortunately, he lived an hour away, and I didn't see him often. We tried talking on the phone, but long-distance calls were prohibitively expensive in those days.

I went to my senior prom with a boy one year younger than me, named Tim. He showed up at my house with his great hair and snappy tux. He confidently fixed my dress right before our pictures. We shook hands at the end of the night. I had no idea he was gay. All I knew was that he felt safe.

Arriving at COLLEGE™ was anticlimactic. My parents drove me four hours north to the small, Catholic university in Duluth, as I was not allowed to have a car my freshman year. They helped carry my baskets and bags of stuff to my dorm room on the second floor, took a look around, handed me a nice greeting card, hugged me and left. As I listened to the other mothers fuss over their daughters, and exclaim and cry, the fathers with their power tools, putting up bunk beds and giving pep talks, I thought about my own parents. How I wished they were different. I read the card after they left, and they surprisingly said they were proud of me. I made my bed and stayed in the room alone until my roommate, Janet, arrived. Then I felt confident enough to prop the door open like the other rooms were doing and wait for other students (mostly older boys, checking out the new possible conquests) to stop by. That's what you do in COLLEGE™.

The school sat atop a very high hill, and you could see Lake Superior if you climbed enough stairs. Duluth was a college town (my Catholic college, St. Scholastica; the University of Minnesota – Duluth; a chiropractic school; probably others) and had everything a college student needed to have a very good time in

1984. I learned almost immediately that the local bars had a well-established Ladies' Night culture, and on certain nights of the week, and we knew the schedule by heart, the bars offered 50-cent or even 25-cent drink specials to the women patrons. These drinks were highly alcoholic, like Long Island iced teas and tequila sunrises that were so full of grenadine we didn't notice the bottom shelf tequila burning the back of our throats. The drinking age in Minnesota was 19, but there were plenty of lenient bouncers, and if you crossed the bridge to Wisconsin, the age was 18. I thought this was maybe how and where I would find a boyfriend.

I made a new best friend right away at COLLEGE™. Lisa was what my parents would have called "wild" or maybe even "loose." She did what she wanted, with whomever she wanted, and I was jealous of her lack of inhibition. With my crippling anxiety, I could never be Lisa. But I felt warm just being in her orbit, watching her move through life seemingly unencumbered by fear, shame, or the wariness I felt every day, in every situation.

On one unseasonably warm night late in late October, during our freshman year, Lisa and I took the city bus to a bar called The Warehouse. As the name suggests, it was previously a warehouse at the Duluth Lake Superior port, with open space, concrete floors, and high ceilings. That place was not especially stringent on checking IDs, depending on which bouncer was at the door, and that made it very popular with college students. After only a few weeks in Duluth, Lisa seemed to already know every bouncer by name, and that night, the one at the door shrugged, smiled, stamped our hands, and let us in. Lisa was a freshman, too, and also didn't have a car, and after Ladies Night, we would not be in any shape for driving anyway. We always took a taxi home to the dorm, splitting the ten-dollar fare. We'd been doing this for a few weeks, and it was fun.

On that night, several drinks in, Lisa recognized one of the guys she had been hooking up with. She waved, and he and his roommate, Steve, came over. Of course, they bought us a drink, at full price. We talked for a few minutes, standing at the plywood bar, drunkenly shouting at each other. Between the pounding music and the hundreds of people in the bar, the noise level was punishing. Lisa and I giggled and went to the bathroom together to touch up our lip gloss. When Lisa's guy offered to bring us to their place for a beer and then drive us home, we took him up on the offer. We were pretty excited about saving ten dollars on cab fare. I figured Lisa and her guy would peel off for the bedroom, and I could hang out and talk to Steve before they drove us back to the dorm. With his awkward manner, pocket t-shirt, and thick-lensed glasses, Steve looked every bit the shy sidekick. I was sure we could stumble through an hour of random conversation. Weather, sports, school. Was he even in school? He looked older. Maybe we could watch TV.

The four of us left the bar, and piled into their car which smelled like old beer and French fries. Soon the radio was blaring a Journey song and we sang along at the top of our lungs. Don't stopppp belieeeeeevingggg! We arrived at their place after a very swervy fifteen-minute drive that felt much longer. Even in my somewhat liquified state, I could see that Lisa's guy wasn't even close to keeping it between the lines, and at one point, he narrowly missed the guardrail – on the other side of the road. I closed my eyes and sang louder.

Their place was an apartment over a garage at the end of a gravel driveway, somewhere in Wisconsin. We climbed the dimly lit rickety wooden stairs and walked in. We were hit with the odor of dirty socks, mildew, and food-caked dishes piled in the sink. Lisa and her guy grabbed a couple of cans of beer from the fridge, and beelined it for the bedroom, closing the door with a soft whump. Steve got us beers, too and I noticed that the light in the fridge was burned out.

We sat on a blue couch in the middle of the small living room. The couch was old and lumpy, and several springs poked the back of my thighs. After the bare minimum of small talk, Steve turned on the old TV, perched on two tan milk crates, with rabbit ear antennas split like grasshopper's legs.

Saturday Night Live was on. We watched the show, laughing at several skits, made much funnier by the drinks we'd consumed. After a while, Steve got me another beer, and scooted closer to me on that crappy blue couch with its wide wooden arms, each large enough to hold a dinner plate. Then he made his move, putting his arm around me and pulling me toward him. He tugged my chin to face him, and kissed me, sloppily with a strong aftertaste of Budweiser. In my mind, I said, whatever. I could make out with this guy, I thought. Especially, since I would get a free ride home from the deal. It was the economic reasoning of a poor college student, and I was willing to use the currency I had.

After a few minutes of kissing me, or whatever that was with his spongy lips, the energy shifted in him, in the room. He shoved me down on the couch, with his knees on either side of my hips. He roughly untucked my white polo shirt, and shoved his hands, callused, with ragged nails, underneath it. He grabbed, pinched, and tugged, like a mine sweeper seeking solid objects, exploding them, and moving on. He eventually tired of that and focused on unbuttoning the camouflage pants I had bought the day before at the Miller Hill Mall. My tequila-soaked brain finally clicked to attention. This guy Steve didn't know that I was waiting until I found the right guy to have official sex with, and he certainly was not that guy. Time slowed down, and my thoughts were looping. I could hear the laugh track on the other television, blaring from the bedroom.

This can't be happening. I'm an adult now. Fight!

I tried to scream, but it only came out as a garbled aaaggghhhhh. I tried to yell, Lisa! Help me! My mouth couldn't form the words, and my tongue was unable to push them out.

I managed to say, "Stop. I don't want to do this! I said

STOP!," but he was focused on pulling my pants down my thighs, workmanlike. I tried to hit him, whack him with my fist, but my fingers were unable to organize, to create a single solid shape.

I tried to shove him off me, but he pushed down my shoulders, and my head banged and banged against the wooden arm of the couch.

There was only the light from the small TV to illuminate the room, this scene, which was the opposite of a still life. I turned my head and watched the gray and white patterns roll over us like a kaleidoscope. I waited for it to be over. I stopped fighting back. I may have tightly closed my eyes like I did when I was a child. Like all those times, I was there, but I wasn't.

He got off me and pulled up his pants. He was still wearing his light brown suede work boots. He fastened his belt, with a heavy oval belt buckle, silver in the TV light. There may have been a horse on it. I don't know how long I laid on the couch, unmoving, staring up at the lightly stained ceiling. Steve sat on the very end of the couch because there was no other furniture. He eventually pointed to the bathroom, "You should get cleaned up." I sat up and found my pants and underwear in a heap on the dusty floor. I pulled them on. I walked across the room and stepped into the tiny bathroom. I closed the white door, thick with coats of paint, the knob old and black. It rattled in my hand. There was a single fixture with one lightbulb on the low ceiling with a pull chain. I pulled it. Surrounding the bulb, was a bright corona of light, and the rest of the small space was a mix of shadows. The baby blue paint on the walls was deeply scuffed in several places. The linoleum was probably once white, but now a mixture of dirty yellow, and blue paint droplets, faded and worn in front of the toilet. I sat down on the cold toilet seat. The ceiling sloped steeply above the toilet, and I had to stoop forward a little.

The honey-slow pace of time was speeding up, and the processing – the room, the pain, what had just happened, was disorienting. The bathroom was freezing, and my teeth started clacking against each other. There were only a few pieces of toilet paper hanging off the brown roll, and I took them and tried to clean myself a little. I noticed there was a button missing from the front of my pants. I rinsed my hands in the once-white sink, heavy rust stains around the drain. It kept dripping after I turned off the faucet. There wasn't any soap. I looked in the round hand mirror hung on the wall with a single nail.

My shock melted, just a little. I got closer to clarity, and I had to consider my options. What was going to happen once I walked out of the bathroom? This was before cell phones, before pagers. I was somewhere in semi-rural Wisconsin. To get to the apartment, we had driven the last few minutes on a gravel road and turned into a gravel driveway. I didn't know Steve's last name. I had not seen a telephone in the apartment, and besides, I didn't think Steve would be thrilled if I dialed 0 or 911 in front of him. I had to get back to the dorm. I opened the bathroom door, stumbled out, and said, "I want to go home." I was probably crying, but my face didn't register tears. The door to the bedroom was still closed, and I figured Lisa would get her own ride back to the dorm. I just couldn't worry about her.

We walked back down those rickety stairs and got into Steve's crappy gold truck, rusty and loud, with cracks in the vinyl seats like fissures in the landscape. We didn't talk. The radio was tuned to the rock station, and it periodically released puffs of crackly, staticky guitar riffs. I sat as close to the passenger door as possible, making myself small. I realized just how much danger I was in. This guy Steve, still drunk and violent, was speeding on the gravel road. I could hear the pinging of rocks hitting the undercarriage of the truck and saw a dull burst of dust behind us in the side mirror. As we pulled onto that long, long bridge that would take me back to Minnesota, time slowed again. I counted the bright lights on the bridge as we went under them, each getting me closer to the end of that night. Steve's amped-up aggression had not completely faded, and an unpleasant smell came off him, earthy and primal. That night, in that gold truck, in a Midwestern October, across that white-lit bridge, was the longest ride of my life. I had yet to feel the relief of survival, and the horror of what happened had not sunk in.

As we neared the college he finally spoke. "I'm leaving for Colorado tomorrow. I won't be back." I still wonder why he told me that. The only words I said were, turn right here. Go up the hill. Pull in there. He stopped in front of the glass door of the dorm lobby. We were under a streetlight, and I took a good look at him. Straight dirty blonde hair, flopped over his forehead, now greasy with sweat. Thick-lensed glasses with gold wire rims. The lenses magnified his watery blue eyes. They were huge, and he blinked slowly, like a frog. He had a small brown mole on his neck. I couldn't look at him anymore. I untied the red bandana that had been knotted at my neck all night. I threw it at him. A souvenir. I got out of the truck and slammed the door.

The next morning, I woke to both a nauseating hangover and a small goose egg on the back of my head. It must have come from hitting my head on the wooden arm of the couch. I made a decision. This was it. This time I would tell.

I slowly walked down the hall and knocked on my RA's door. When she answered, I told her what happened, and asked if I should go to the police. We went to see the director of residential life instead, whose only job was to keep us safe. After I shakily recounted the evening's events, she just shook her head. "You need to accept responsibility. You drank too much in a bar. You left the bar with two men you didn't know. What did you think was going to happen? Maybe next time, you'll make better decisions." No police report. No doctor. Not even a notation in her spiral notebook. Just an admonishment by a disinterested, judgmental nun.

I left her office, numb, and found Lisa. She shrugged her

shoulders. "It happens. Get one of those free pregnancy tests at the Student Health Center." This was several years before we knew that straight people could get AIDS, and pregnancy should have been the least of my worries. Later that week, Lisa told me that the guy she slept with that night gave her crabs, and she laughed. Soon enough he would find out that Lisa gave him herpes. Lisa went to The Warehouse the next weekend, the weekend after that, and the weekend after that, with another friend.

Something cracked apart in me that night. I was nearly irretrievably broken. It was like my emotional pilot light had been extinguished, and I could no longer kindle joy or connection. I never went back to The Warehouse. It was years before I could drive over that bridge without holding my breath.

In fact, after that night, I developed a bridge phobia. Even now, I need to count in my head the entire time crossing a bridge span. My jaw clenches and I start to sweat. More often than not, I'm taken back to that night in October. I don't know if that will ever stop.

As a child, I had hoped, thought, and even assumed that once I was an adult, things would get easier, and I would feel safe. I would be big and strong. I would fight back and things would be okay. That night crossing the bridge I realized that being an adult offered no protection. I had sorely overestimated my power. With that hope taken away, I began my tailspin.

It's Called The Lingual Frenulum

Our dorm rooms at St. Scholastica were spartan and had what we would call today, a neutral palette. There were two twin beds, two wooden desks, and wood-like built-in shelves, in the shade of lightly-burned toast. In some rooms, enterprising dads had built their kids sturdy bunks to increase the meager floor space. Our room did not have bunks. The walls were white, and the curtains were a sickly, milky shade of tan and made of thick vinyl. The floors in our rooms were shiny brown, with some commercial finish that made it impervious to anything that might spill on it.

My first roommate, Janet, and I were distorted mirror images of each other. She attended 13 years of Catholic school and wore cable sweaters, lace collars, and puffy Laura Ashley floral dresses. Janet was organized, and tidy - she brought a huge plastic caddy of cleaning supplies to college - and had a high moral code. When something offended her, she pursed her thin lips tightly and wrinkled her long, pointed nose. As a good passive-aggressive Minnesotan, she never actually said anything to me, just silently judged. I moved in hours before she did, and hung up my "Born in the USA" poster that prominently featured Springsteen's jean-clad butt. The first weekend on campus, I was invited to my first COLLEGE™ party, and I was thrilled to go. I came home from that party at the same time Janet was leaving for Mass. She told me she was about to call the police and report me as a missing person. I called her "Dammit Janet" behind her back.

After arriving at COLLEGE™, my magical boyfriend scenario did not materialize, even though I tried so hard. I had no idea what a healthy relationship looked like, even after closely observing others on campus. I tried everything. I changed my hairstyle again. I wore more makeup. I bought trendy clothes I could not afford. I constantly studied the popular girls, to figure out what they had/did that made them so likable, so admired. But, I could not see the fog of neediness that shrouded me. How clingy I was. How starved I was for compliments, for any scrap of attention. I wore my damage like a second skin; everyone except me could see it.

In the dorm, the lounge on each floor, with couches and a TV was our social hub. On the weekends, the boys took over the lounge to watch football and talk shit about the teams. They were loud and crude and were constantly telling the girls, grab me another beer, wouldya, followed by a slap on the ass, no matter which girl volunteered. The boys would laugh. Boys will be boys, I thought. Given my history, their behavior was not particularly off-putting, and I was fine, happy even, when my butt was the one that got smacked. I held my breath, just waiting for someone to take notice of me. To like me.

Some evenings in the lounge, I overheard the older girls speaking in low tones. It did not take me long to decipher the topic; it jarred my bones the first time I understood what they were talking about. I never had the vocabulary to talk about abuse and assault, like these girls. If it hadn't happened to them, it happened to their roommate or best friend. Because guys just couldn't control themselves. In a sick way, maybe it was a college rite of passage. One more toll to pay for being a young woman.

    I had never heard anyone talking about women's bodies and violations like that. Even when my parents sent me to a psychiatrist, when my eating disorder was steadily dismantling and dissolving my body, I did not dare disclose anything about the abuse I had endured. First of all, he never asked. Second, why would I tell a man, wearing a cliché tweed blazer, sitting too close to me, what other men had done to my young body? I did not want to give him any ideas, in that dim room, alone with him, with the door closed.

    I was shocked at how comfortable those girls felt talking about such dark topics, only pausing when one of the boys walked through the lounge, bouncing a basketball or kicking a hacky sack. In hushed, even reverent voices, they would say things like, did you hear about Jackie? She knows the guy who did it but is too scared to say anything. She's gotta stop wearing those skirts when she goes out. She needs to stop looking, you know, available.

    I had few real friends that freshman year and I could not imagine having that type of conversation with any of them. The only person I could talk to was Lisa. Even after what happened that night we went to The Warehouse, we remained friends. We were underage, but we were crafty. We would sometimes dress up in our nicest clothes on a weeknight, thinking we looked like real business ladies, and take the bus to happy hour at the Holiday Inn or the Radisson hotel. We sometimes ordered a drink, if there was a friendly bartender, but mostly we went for the free buffet. Meatballs and chicken wings always tasted extra good when they were free. When Lisa was low on cash, she would procure a usually married "date" at the Holiday Inn or the bar at the Radisson. When her new friend looked in his wallet after Lisa left their hotel room, it would be lighter. According to her, no one ever complained. She also had a thing for the drummers who performed on weekends at those hotels. She would meet them after their sets were done at closing time, and there would always be a little money on the dresser for her, and sometimes a tiny vial of cocaine.

  I wouldn't say Lisa was happy-go-lucky, but she was brazen. She used clouds of Aquanet to tease up her long, wavy red hair, wore heavy black eyeliner around her bright green eyes, and knew how to rock a miniskirt. And, she was fun. She always called me her "little scaredy cat." I learned so many things from her, after that night at The Warehouse. How to hit a guy in the nose, or successfully knee him in the nuts, if things went sideways. What to order on a restaurant menu, if your "date" was paying. Which drinks you could pretty safely combine with which drugs. How to run in high heels.

  While I didn't exactly trust her, because I didn't trust

anyone, I cautiously shared a few things about myself, and she never judged me. She sensed my neediness and it didn't put her off. She was my kindred guiding spirit in many ways. When I felt brave enough, often after we had been drinking, to let slip a detail about a childhood experience, she was matter-of-fact about it. Nonchalant. Accepting. Her own childhood had been filled with violence, drugs, abuse, and poverty. Nothing I told her was any worse than what had happened to her. She managed to completely normalize my experiences that were anything but normal, and at that time, I was grateful.

I was an anxious, constantly triggered, depressed mess. The undiagnosed PTSD from the abuse and the assault filled me with a persistent and deep terror. I had somehow reasoned that what I experienced was because I had let my guard down. I had failed. I started keeping a kitchen knife under my mattress. I found the exits in every room. I had constant conflict between longing to be desired, and the need to protect myself at all costs. It was exhausting.

But, there was only one thing I found, quite by accident, that could reliably distract my agitated mind. As counterintuitive as it sounds, taking risks and engaging in daring or dangerous behavior, on a small or large scale, was the true antidote to my anxiety. It was the only thing that quieted those out-of-control, squirrelly what-if thoughts. It was like fighting fire with a bigger fire. Besides weed and alcohol, this was likely the worst, and yet the best, coping mechanism I came up with. I avoided those anxious, jabbing thoughts by thinking about and planning and doing other things. My brain see-sawed between anxiety and action. I was trying to strong-arm some control over my body, thoughts, and behavior because the buzz of anxiety sometimes made me feel physically sick.

This wasn't the first time I had gone down this road. In high school, I would crawl out my bedroom window after my parents had gone to sleep, and meet my friends at the end of the block, where they were waiting with the headlights off. We would coast down the hill in Holly's beat-up Chevy or Amanda's borrowed Pontiac. The sneaking out got so bad my father nailed my window shut. During the lunch hour in tenth grade, my older friends and I drove over the bridge from Minnesota into Wisconsin, slammed a couple of shots at a bar that never carded, and then got back before the lunch bell rang. I kept a small Tylenol bottle filled with vodka in my locker. My eating disorder was jumbled up in there as well. The less of me there was, the more people liked me. My pointy hipbones and skeletal ribs finally bought their approval.

After the assault, I spent the rest of the fall semester trying to survive. I had nightmares about driving off that long bridge between Superior, Wisconsin, and Duluth and drowning in the cold lake. I would wake up choking, the front of my t-shirt soaked in sticky sweat. I dreamed my hair was on fire, and I was running from room to room in an old house, looking for water. I dreamed I was being chased by a man, backstage at a theatre. I ran up a ladder, and when the faceless man grabbed my ankle, I twisted around, showed him the butcher knife in my hand, jumped off the ladder, and stabbed him over and over. The sensation was like sticking a fork into an underdone and bony steak. My body felt that overly real sensation many nights, mostly in the confusing time between sleeping and waking. Many mornings when I woke up, my right hand was curled in a fist, in front of my chest. I don't remember ever feeling bad about stabbing the man.

Something dark and vast had cracked open inside me, and I tried my best to fill it with food, drugs, alcohol, shopping, spending money earmarked for textbooks on nights out, and cheap earrings. I eventually hooked up with a couple of shy guys I knew from the dorm, who I could count on to be decent to me. And they were. They were grateful I made my body available to them. They demanded nothing else from me.

I half fell in love with a beautiful boy, with green eyes the color of the bottom of a lake, who went to school at another college, an hour away, in Wisconsin. I felt protected when I was with him, and when he held my hand, I felt calm for the first time since I was small. We saw each other several times, each date ending with a chaste kiss. When we got back from Christmas break, I wondered out loud to my friends how Alex could be so kind, such a gentleman. They began to cackle. 'Cuz he's gay, you dummy! I was shocked, then embarrassed that I had unwittingly been duped, or more likely just ignored the signs and duped myself. Just like with my date to the senior prom. But mostly, I was really sad. I told Alex all this, and he offered to be friends, but I felt too humiliated. I had to cast the mooring line off my one safe refuge and drift.

The anxiety raced around my mind with so many messages that I was fearful I was going crazy. But my mind also saved me. When the swirl got to be too much, some other part of my brain sprang to life: Hey! Look over here! Ooh! This could be super fun! Let's do this other thing!

I started going to parties in unfamiliar places, with people I didn't know. I flirted, hard, with a guy. Then, I'd say, bye! and walk away. I was accused of being a cock tease. I rode in cars with people I knew were drunk. I procrastinated on my coursework and would fuel up with No-Doz, and work through the entire night. I smoked sometimes, mostly to look cool. On really bad days, I compulsively binged on pizza and Baskin Robbins ice cream, and tried, mostly unsuccessfully, not to purge. Throwing up was horrible, but getting fat was worse.

I had completely lost my way. I tried to find my way back in anonymous tangled sheets, and at a short-lived job at a deli downtown, where I was paid in cash, and mocked for not being Jewish. I started to eat and couldn't stop. I would stare into the bottom of bowl after bowl of breakfast cereal, with its agreeable crunch as it broke down between my molars, and slid down my throat, the artificial colors and sugar feeding my tired brain and body. I gained weight. It didn't matter.

By February, my grades were slipping, and I was in danger of losing my scholarship. My performance in my senior year of high school had been outstanding, full of trophies and certificates, and small scholarships. I received one large scholarship, from the Catholic Order of the Benedictines, that covered almost a quarter of my tuition. Federal student loans and the small handouts from my grandmothers paid for room and board, and the rest of the tuition. If I lost that scholarship, due to bad grades, I would never get it back, and I could not afford to attend the next year. I would either have to quit college or transfer to a state school, maybe even have to move back home. Part of me felt the deep angst of that situation. Part of me was just numb and could not find the energy to care.

My roommate Janet finally moved to a different room, because she was tired of being woken up when I came home at all hours and when I'd scream during those nightmares. She was a teetotaler and hated the reek of booze I brought into the room, and the boys I occasionally snuck in, even though they were always gone by daybreak.

As spring arrived, I finally was able to make an effort to get myself together. I turned 19. I went home for spring break and acted like everything was fine. I put most of the pieces of myself back together with twine, tape, and some shaky optimism. It had been months since the assault, and things were starting to feel more normal, or what passed for normal. I had fewer nightmares. I thought about that night in the apartment over the garage less and less.

In early May, the anticipation of springtime came to Duluth. The snow was mostly gone, and the weather warmed to 50 degrees. It felt glorious and cheerful, after six months of winter. We put beach towels and blankets on the semi-thawed grass. We sprawled in our shorts and our sweatshirts, attempting to get tan, Rayban sunglasses perched on our noses.

Every year, the college held a spring dance, right before the frenzy of cramming for finals, so that we could blow off a little steam. It was a relief to have something to look forward to. That year's theme was "The 50's," so the organizers and attendees tried their best to recreate a sock hop. Mostly, we looked like ridiculous rejects from the movie Grease. Some students made an effort: there were a few "nerds" with white-taped plastic glasses, bow ties, and high-waisted pants. A few guys wore their high school letter jackets and rolled their jeans at the ankle. Some girls wore headbands, bright pink lipstick, and flowered dresses they bought at Goodwill.

The night of the dance, I entered the event space. After paying five dollars and getting my hand stamped, I was hit with the chemical scents of attraction. Dousings of Drakkar Noir, lemony Jean Naté, and Calvin Klein Obsession fogged the room and competed with copious amounts of Aquanet and Vidal Sassoon styling gel. The second sensory wave hit: Loud music from multiple speakers, and a hundred young people shouting to be heard, some of them already slurring their words.

I was proud of my outfit, and it was somewhat authentic. I had stayed with my grandmother the summer after tenth grade, after my tall, horrible grandfather died, and one day, we dug around in the locked shed in the backyard. Under layers of magazines and old purses, we came across a stash of fabric that my grandmother had kept for the thirty years since my Aunt Karen was in high school. Miraculously, the mice and other critters had left it alone. My grandmother sewed me a calf-length circle skirt of crisp, black cotton with a cute and colorful Lady & The Tramp pattern. Together we also made a hand-tooled leather belt to wear with it, and once everything was completed, I stood in the middle of her tiny living room and twirled and twirled, while Eddy Arnold and Gene Autry crooned from the 8-track player. She clapped, pleased that her work was appreciated. I had brought that skirt and belt to college with me, thinking I might have an occasion to wear it.

The DJ played songs by Fats Domino and Chubby Checker, the Coasters, and Richie Valens. Many of the dancers could not figure out how to dance to the songs, especially the fast ones, so they gyrated their hips and flapped their elbows, like chickens. For the slow songs, the "clutch and sway" method was the most prevalent. I stood by myself, and drank vodka-spiked red punch from a red Solo cup, both wanting someone to ask me to dance and also relieved I was not out on the floor. My parents were big fans of 50's music, and I learned how to do the Twist and a half-decent Jitterbug from my mother, in the kitchen. But I didn't want to be the only weirdo out there who knew the moves.

As I was sipping my very strong, very sweet drink, I noticed the school's star soccer player, David, checking me out. He was hanging out with his jock buddies, and he smiled at me a few times. Then he strolled over, jeans cuffed, white t-shirt, collar popped on his brown leather jacket. When he came to me, his hand extended, it was like being warmed by the sun. This didn't happen to girls like me, who weren't quite pretty enough, who were never really popular, who could never quite figure out how to fit in, and I was glowing. I was so flattered he had chosen me. David, with his milk chocolate skin, his wide white smile, his slightly bow-legged gait from muscular legs, and years of riding horses. Would we dance to a fast song or a slow one? A fast one might be better since I was a couple of inches taller than him, and I didn't want him to feel uncomfortable.

David took my hand, but instead of going out on the dance floor, he steered me through the double doors and out into the bright hallway. We headed toward his dorm room. He said, *it's more private there.* In my mind, I was anticipating what it was going to be like. We would talk about TV shows, music, and what we wanted to do after college. I didn't know him well, and I was excited that he was interested in me, and wanted to get to know me.

In that moment, it felt like things were finally turning around. That everything was going to be okay. As we rounded the corner to his room, he told me that he was planning to stay at the dance, but he saw me and thought, "Why not! You're totally into me, I can tell. Why not!" He grinned, confident and wolfish. He opened the door for us, then grabbed a sock from the floor and put it on the outside door handle. The universal man-code signal for I've got a girl in here. Get lost. He closed the door.

He suggested that we sit on his bed, the lower bunk, because it would be comfortable. I was starting to get the feeling that what he was expecting and what I was expecting were two very different things. I said sitting on the floor on his big pillows would be fine. I said, "Maybe you can put on some music." He got up, and then an album by Chicago started playing. He had a green banker's lamp on his desk, and he turned it on and put a thin white t-shirt over it. Is this mood lighting? Weird, I thought.

We sat down on the cushions and talked for a couple of minutes. Then he put his hand on the back of my head, pulled me forward, and kissed me. Hard. It was less like kissing, and more like him mashing his teeth against my lips. At first, I thought he was just really bad at kissing. But, he did it again. I didn't respond, I tried to pull away from him. He was hurting me. He forced my mouth open and began to suck my tongue, pulling it. He didn't stop. I remember the moment when I felt something tear inside my mouth. David, the star athlete, was strong and he was rough. David was also determined. I didn't stand a chance. He left thumb-sized bruises inside my forearms and red marks where he twisted my wrists. He sucked a huge purple hickey into the side of my neck. He sunk a deep, mouth-shaped bruise into my shoulder, complete with small teeth marks, above my right collarbone. I was later glad he did not quite break the skin.

During those minutes, I was once again both deeply present and deeply dissociated from my body. The things were happening to my flesh, being done to my flesh, but my mind traveled elsewhere, to a place that had never been mapped. It was like having one foot on the brake and one foot on the gas. The sensation of moving forward and backward at the same time, yet not moving at all. The feeling of being a solid, a liquid, and a gas, unsure of which I would be when it was over.

When it was over, David stood and told me I had to leave. He was going back to the dance. He checked to make sure the ink stamp was still on his hand, so he could get back in. He didn't want to pay another five dollars. I don't remember how I got back to my dorm room.

I sat on my bed that night, in my single room, dazed, bruised, mouth bleeding, skirt sticky. I couldn't register what had happened, at first, why I hurt everywhere, especially my mouth. David gave me a corporal souvenir that May night. He had pulled my tongue so violently that he ripped the webbed ridge of tissue underneath, that tethers the tongue to the floor of my mouth. It's called the lingual frenulum. My mouth took weeks to heal and I could barely eat.

Years later, in a session with my therapist, Pat, I could only access rage and shame, and spit out the most generic description of what happened, like it was lifted from the pages of a how-to manual, "Rape for Beginners." Steps one through ten. My description was mechanical. Removed. Rote. Sanitized.

At some point, Pat interrupted me. She intuitively knew I remembered far more details than I was letting on. She gently told me that being aware of what was happening during the time of trauma and letting myself remember was important. It could help me process. It could help me heal. When she told me that, I got up from her hard blue couch, furious, and paced the small room, with its dim lighting and boxes of tissues. Remember? I want to forget it. All of it. When my anger cooled, I sat back down and she said, "Go to that night - what do you remember? Go there and stay there for as long as you can."

I took a breath. I wasn't sure I was ready, or if I was ever going to be ready, but I had to try. Looking into the middle distance, twisting a tissue between my thumb and forefinger, I went back, as if watching a video that had been curiously rewound to that night.

The Terminator poster above the desk.

The Special Export beer cans stacked in a pyramid on the windowsill.

The cold brown epoxy floor.

The sound of guys playing a game of Nerf football in the hallway.

David's breath, flat, sour from beer and mouth breathing.

A textbook lying with its belly on the desk, its cover and back exposed, surrendered.

My right shoe, a black flat, in front of the cushions. The left shoe still on my foot.

While all of this was extraordinarily painful to extract, like splinters from a wound, she explained I was fortunate. That I remembered, that I felt what it was like to be there. That I had acted. That I did not suffer "dislocation of expectation" in the moment. This is when the brain tries to compare the current, traumatic situation with an experience from the past. The frontal lobe continually loops, like a record player, stuck on the last groove of the album, trying and failing to find a similar situation to work from. When this happens, the body freezes and waits for directions from the brain. This is the "deer in headlights" phenomenon.

That wasn't the case for me, on that May night. I did not freeze. I was there. And while David was doing those things to my body, my brain was processing with speed, using the full playbook from what happened to me seven months before, back in October. My brain had assembled the next steps to take.

My brain said: Say stop. I did and David barked out a laugh.

My brain said: Try to scream. I did and David put his sweaty hand over my mouth.

My brain said: Okay, try to fight him. I tried to scratch him. He captured my wrists and twisted.

My brain said: Move your shoulders, get away. FIGHT! I did, and then, angry, David bit me.

He said something to me after he did that, but I can't remember what it was. Something like, you know you like it. My brain was furiously trying to recalibrate, but the playbook was useless that night because the rules had changed.

I didn't report the assault, because no one would believe me. I knew better. I had seen what had happened to a couple other girls that year when they had told friends they were assaulted by athletes. When they went to campus authorities. Word got around. I would be accused of making up the assault, just to get attention. Or I would be accused of "morning after" remorse. He was a celebrated athlete, and it was not like I was popular. If by chance other students believed me, they wouldn't care. Neither would the administration. After what had happened in October, I learned the wisdom of keeping my mouth shut.

My friends saw the bruises but never mentioned them. I wore a turtleneck in May to hide my neck. With less than a month left in the school year, we were exhausted from the tolls and taxes and the price of admission that we constantly paid for being female and being alive on that college campus. We were continually overlooked academically and politically, even though women were the seventy-five percent majority on campus. We did not complain. We constantly adjusted our makeup, our clothes, and our personalities, rounding our edges to fill the mold of acceptable and capable. We worried about being aggressive – no one wanted to be called a bitch, a ballbreaker. We had to be attractive enough, but not overly tempting. There were many rumors about two of the middle-aged male professors and the many problems they had with being easily tempted. Those girls in no way earned an "easy A."

Collectively, as women, we had lost any passion we had for supporting one another. We just didn't have any words left. We retreated, quietly waiting out the last few weeks of the school year. Then we moved out of the dorm and went back to where we came from to heal.

That terrible night with David happened decades ago. I still pull it from my memory periodically, to examine it like a relic. There are other times that night pops up accidentally before I can manage it. Recently, I went to a new dentist, and he asked questions about the anatomy of my mouth. My tongue. He mentioned it was somewhat unusual. After he removed the little mirror from my mouth, I blurted out that it was an old injury, from a sexual assault. Over the years I had practiced saying that out loud, but had never done so. The dentist looked at me with pity and confusion in his eyes. The lower half of his face was covered by a white mask, so I could not see if he was trying to form words with his mouth. He did not ask any more questions.

For years I'd been ruminating on survivorship and how my childhood abuse and those assaults in October and May stained the many good things in my life that came later. Relationships, motherhood, travel, work. I assumed that frog-eyed Steve was long gone to Colorado, but I wished there was a rape survivors database I could search that would help me find David, and see where he was. Maybe he lived five states away. Maybe his crime(s) caught up to him, and he was in prison. Or perhaps he died in his in his twenties or thirties. Any of those outcomes would have been fine with me. I wanted to know that he was never coming near me. If he were still alive, he would be in his fifties. Would I recognize him if I ran into him at the grocery store? I was unsure.

Then last year, on a summer Saturday, I was driving around running errands near my house. I decided to stop by Fleet Farm and pick up a gift card for a friend. As I pulled into a parking place in the big asphalt lot, I looked over and saw a man coming out of the store entrance, white and orange bags in each hand. He was close enough that I could see him clearly, but far enough away that he would not catch me staring, mouth agape, face burning. He was balding, his brown scalp naked above his forehead, and the start of a paunch strained the buttons on his plaid shirt. I recognized that bow-legged walk even after all these years. I must have put my car in park. I don't remember doing it. Everything was silent, and I could only hear the whooshing in my ears.

David. I had imagined this moment dozens, maybe hundreds of times over the years. There were many possible scenarios I planned to unleash when I saw him, all of them dramatic, many of them violent. I would hurl myself at him, scream obscenities, scream, RAPIST, RAPIST, RAPIST! Or, gun the engine of my car, plow into him, and watch him tumble over the hood. Laugh. But the moment I saw him at Fleet Farm was nothing like that. I was unprepared. My throat tightened like it had that night. My mouth knew to ache, and the skin on my neck was gooseflesh like it was trying to get away this time.

I tried to scream like I had tried that night, but all that came out was a dusty, ohmygod. I tried over and over to harness my voice, as I watched David saunter, carefree, white and orange bags swinging, from the front of the store to the hulk of his shiny black truck, so big it looked like he would need a step stool to get into the cab. The sun reflected sharply off the chrome bumper, and I had to tilt my head to avoid the laser-like light.

My mind and body felt disconnected, like a snake sawed in half. My body braced for action, while my brain buzzed and clicked, searching for the right frequency, and the sequence that would order my body to move. It was him. After all these years, it was him.

After more deep breaths, I was able to reorient myself to this time, this life, this person I am now. I heard him slam the driver's door on the truck, only a few rows away. His door was just out of my vision, and I saw it in my mind's eye. The engine started, and I heard the sound of the exaggerated exhaust as he backed up and pulled away.

I pressed the button to start my car, completely forgetting about the gift card. I backed out of the parking spot and circled the parking lot, over and over to see where he may have gone. I could not find him. I drove through that neighborhood, for minutes or maybe it was hours, thinking he might live nearby. I didn't see the truck. I could not find him. My tremoring hands gripped the wheel, and I drove home, taking the side streets, in case I had to pull over. All the while I was running the film of what had happened hours away from here, decades earlier.

I made it home and parked in the garage. I walked into the house, turned off the beeping alarm, and walked down the hall to my office. I sat down on my black office chair, touched my phone screen, and on some type of autopilot, searched for David on Facebook. I had never looked for him before. I found him easily. He was unconcerned about privacy. I started scrolling through his posts, and his photos. He was twice divorced. He had five children and a granddaughter.

I thought I would feel anger. I thought I would feel the intensity of the violation over and over. I thought I would feel guilty or sad or frustrated that I hadn't done anything when I saw him. That I didn't make him pay. That I failed. That I let him get away. But I didn't feel any of those things. I felt weirdly calm, which scared me. I felt okay. What the hell was happening?

I continued scrolling, and I saw what he had posted just a couple of weeks earlier. Just two white words, all caps, against a dark blue background: Why Not?? My body felt it before my brain did, and I sensed a splash of vomit in the back of my throat. That post took me right back to that May night. Why Not?? I can't remember what he was referring to in his post, and it didn't matter. I had to close my eyes, and think of happier things, like my therapist Pat had taught me. The beach. My kids.

Then I scrolled again through more of his Facebook posts. I couldn't stop. There he was, smiling, holding his granddaughter. Smiling, holding a wriggling fish. Smiling, shaking some guy's hand, clutching a certificate in a frame. It started to feel like too much. What I was seeing, innocuous David, family man David, clashed violently with the David I knew. The David I experienced. The details of that night finally came to me, at me, like angry bees, in search of a victim. This must be what being triggered feels like, I thought. I closed my eyes, put my palms on my knees, and took a breath – in through the nose, out through the mouth. I calmed down a little.

I opened my eyes. I knew that whatever this was, whatever was happening was big. It was important. I didn't understand it, but this time I was going to choose to be brave. I picked up my cell phone again and looked at David's profile photo, really looked at it, one more time. I had to. Nowhere in his profile does he mention being a soccer player-rapist.

I clicked the phone screen closed. Then, I opened the screen and looked at him again, and closed the screen. Again. And again. I don't know how many times I repeated that ritual. I waited and assessed my body. The nausea was mostly gone. My heart rate had slowed. The sweat had stopped leaking into my damp shirt. I weirdly felt… nothing. Nothing as in, meh. Nothing. I assessed my body again. I felt no quickening or trembling or tightening. My heart was still fairly calm and rhythmic. My brain seemed to be processing at a normal speed. I felt the office chair under my thighs and the plastic carpet protector under my bare feet.

I felt empty, unburdened like I had just rid my body of a parasite. As if I had removed a cancerous organ. But underneath, I think I also felt a loss. I had been carrying David around with me for decades. He and what he had done to me was so deeply a part of my story, of my fabric, my mythology. Who would I be, who would I become without him? Would I recover?

All I knew that day was that I felt light. I felt clean. I said I'm letting you go.

POSTCARDS FROM THE ROAD

PART I

I-40

Dear Rudy:

    There was a night, years ago, when we drove from Amarillo to Albuquerque, long before the days of having a world map in your pocket. We had to stop by the side of the road and check the atlas, splayed out before us like a blanket, like a sacred text, like communion between one place and another. The dome light was yellow and weak and we couldn't tell the difference between a green line and a blue one, off-shooting the interstate and into the dusty desert. I had wanted to stop at the wayside rest and you said, "No. I didn't like the way those guys were looking at you back at the truck stop." You said this as you put my hand on your zipper, maybe to break the monotony of the murmur of tires on pavement, their tongues licking the lane markers as we rolled on.

    On the previous trip to Amarillo, when we dropped off your little boy from your first marriage, we ate steak at the Big Texan with its neon sign, the huge cow in the parking lot, and photos of celebrities on the wall. That's when I still ate meat and you still had money. That's when you drank four Lone Star beers, one bottle after the other, and told me I was crazy when I asked you if I should drive. That's when you left those bruises on the inside of my arm. On the side of my neck. That's when you whispered, "You're just a stupid bitch who doesn't know her place." I wondered if love and pain were always two halves of a whole.

On the night of the truck stop, the rest stop, the map, it took us five hours by interstate, highway, and backroad to get to Albuquerque from Amarillo. On these trips, you liked to take the "scenic route." I liked to count the green mile marker numbers on the interstate as they flagged our progress and the passing of time. I got to maybe the 33rd marker before you noticed I was no longer listening to you, and in a single swift move, you yanked the back of my hair to get me to pay attention. That night, it felt like staged scenes appeared wherever the headlights could slice through the darkness, like a dull blade. We saw a coyote, thin, with a sharp nose and sandy fur lope crookedly along the road. I spotted more than one armadillo and wondered what it felt like not to have one's soft parts always exposed.

As we drove, fine sand gritted between my molars. On those backroads on that night, there was no cadence, no metronome of miles or minutes, just a syncopated waltz full of flat notes and night noises. There was just the darkness, the map, the sound of your breathing, the thud of wheels as they lost contact with the uneven asphalt, and the ringing in my ears as I strained to hear your thoughts before you thought them.

A Bible Story

Dear Phil:

In the beginning, I noticed how those fine lines crinkled around your eyes when you smiled. In the beginning, you smiled a lot. You were so handsome, in that way people call "rugged." Time and experience had revised the smooth landscape of your face and body. The spot on your right shoulder had a texture like soft fur. From the time you dumped your motorcycle, you said. Your left knee had three small white stripes of a scar, if one looked closely. In the beginning, I thought that thin scar running through your left eyebrow was sexy.

    I spotted you first. You came into that 50s place in Albuquerque one night when I was bartending. You walked in with my friend Tom and sat at the bar. I was wearing a white shirt with an ugly red bowtie. I was supposed to wear a paper hat, but that was too ridiculous. You ordered a drink—I think it was a gin & tonic. I liked the sound of your voice, and you left me a decent tip. You were a friend-of-a-friend-of-a-friend. You had references, I checked. I thought maybe you could be the refuge from the mess my life had become. You were so different from the boys I had known at the university.

    I slowly eased into your orbit, joining "your guys," men, really, and their girlfriends who coalesced into a protective screen around you. I listened to you speak of your deep faith, and I thought, maybe he's a good one. Perhaps I didn't think that at all, rather I may have thought, wow, he's hot. I wonder if he's single. Or single enough.

In the beginning, you were such a gentleman, Southern gentleman, you would correct me. You often carried your tiny Bible in your back pocket, and would laugh, "Don't worry, I'm not here to convert you." Even if that was true, you kept Bible verses on the tip of your tongue, like spears. Sometimes, you'd deploy them during our conversations.

That was in the beginning, and it was good. You were an adult man, and my 21-year-old self was impressed. You cooked me salmon and steaks and acted like adult boyfriends on TV. We would spend Saturday mornings lying in bed, drinking coffee if you didn't get called into work at the trucking company, and we dreamed of all the places we would travel. I had studied abroad in Ireland, but you had never been out of the country, not even to Mexico. That seemed to irritate you a little. I seemed to irritate you a little.

I started going to church with you on Sundays, once in a while. Then I started going with you every week. The long sermons about women obeying their husbands and all the available celestial punishments made me uncomfortable. Once, as I was leaving a service, a woman made a snippy comment about me wearing pants to church. I had not cracked the code of what it meant to be a woman, your woman in the context of your church. You said you were going to help me.

You and God didn't have a problem with me sleeping at your place most nights. It was easier than having you call me every night when I was at my place, and ask, "Who's there with you?" Or have you show up at my little studio apartment and pound on the brown steel door until I answered. You were not Jesus, wanting to come in and forgive my sins.

The woman who lived next door gave me a small, sad smile when I saw her in the laundry room. Once, you were pretty out of control and bellowed in front of my locked door that you had a knife, and that you were coming back with a gun. I stood on my balcony, shaking. Above me, my neighbor, the cop was grilling. I could smell the chicken and green peppers on his little hibachi, and hear the clank of beer bottles being set on concrete. He yelled down and said it was sounding a little rough at my place. He asked if I wanted him to call it in. "No, it will be fine. He's just had a rough week."

Damage knows damage, and you soaked into my pores like fragrant oil, warm and familiar, and bled the hope from my bones. You were the wolf sleeping with the lamb, in a queen-sized bed. You had become your own character in the Old Testament, announcing decrees and punishments, like a modern King Harrod. When I saw your jaw working, that vein pumping in your temple, I knew that your release, your version of the Promised Land was just ahead.

Driving to church in your clean red car, Sunday after Sunday, I was not allowed to change the radio station, even though I detested country music, or at least I thought I did. Before I met you. You sprained my index finger once, yanking it backward when I absentmindedly reached over to turn up the volume. Your "corrections" always came swiftly, delivered with slaps and chapter and verse on everything I did wrong. I had given up saying, please stop. I had given up saying, please don't. I had given up saying, I didn't mean it.

Still, you were my savior, delivering me from evil, until you weren't. I realized that I was no longer worshiping a higher power in order to be saved. I was worshiping you, and praying I would not be destroyed. One day, I woke up, and for no particular reason, I was done being crucified. I tried explaining this to you, using my secular language, and you didn't or claimed you didn't understand. But, now I'm using your Bible, with all its words and stories, to explain.

Start with this: Like the Apostle Paul, the scales fell from my eyes and I was ready to believe. Just not in you. You had written your own commandments and consequences, filled with words like submit, and repent, and told me all the time that you're the one God had chosen to cast out my demons. You gaslit me. You're a false prophet. You convinced me I was the sinner, the unclean one.

You curated your group of disciples, "your guys," men like you who loved Jesus, beer, and football, and worshiped your message of faith, loyalty, and retribution. There were more than twelve, and they sat with you for supper, as they knew it wouldn't be the last. They were there to hear you share The Good News.

But, then… the day came, and I could see you so clearly. You collected my misdeeds, my "transgressions," and pulled them behind you like battle chains dragging in the dust. You said I invited Satan into my heart, and you taunted me for being so weak. I knew when you were coming for me, red-faced, lips pursed, breathing heavily, nostrils flared like a horse before a race. I thought, tell me, are you using your fists to drive out Satan, or to punish me for letting him in? Your apologies to me later were thin, transitory, like confessing to the passing wind. There were bruises and injuries I couldn't cover with makeup, especially in the heat of the Albuquerque summer. You came clean to your believers about what you did (again) and the mask you showed them was a study in contrition: "I guess I got carried away, boys, I'll have to pray about it." In truth, I was the only one praying. Praying for deliverance.

That upstairs neighbor was my angel in a black shirt and a badge, that night you said you were going to send me to hell where I belonged. You'd been drinking, way more than usual. The puffed lip, and the bruises that tattooed my ribs and wrists, told the story when you were finally forced to open the door. You were a three-striker. Not that it mattered in the late 1980s. You were sentenced to a 30-day exile, not in the desert, but behind bars. You sent me impassioned letters about how remorseful you were, and how things were going to be different this time. I was the love of your life. I was the only one that could help you be the man of God you wanted to be. I was the only one who could quiet your urges, and make you gentle and tender. You were nothing without me by your side. You begged me for forgiveness. Each letter was more desperate than the one before it. I did not write back. I did not accept your calls, the mechanical voice informing me the call was collect from a correctional facility. I could feel you seething from six miles away.

When you were released more than ten days early, I did not drive your red car to pick you up. You made me pay. You had learned nothing during your exile but terrifying new ways to use your fists. You were brimming with arrogance and maybe, as you said, the full power of the Holy Spirit. Who knows? You were convinced you could part the seas for the unbelievers and lead them to redemption. You were convinced you could do a lot of things. I looked forward to seeing you try to part those seas and drown. And you did, in your own way, when three strikes became four, and you went to prison.

John 8:36: …if the Son sets you free, you will be free indeed.

All that remained, after everything, was for me to cast off your chains, and unravel your doctrine and dogma. I knew it by heart; every word had been pounded into me. As I started to heal, I dismantled it, page by page, verse by verse. I rearranged the pile of your words, parables, and psalms, into stories of joy, life, and forgiveness. I would hide my light no more.

I had to say goodbye to you, and your toxic brand of religion that was a tangled mess of love and violence, redemption and hatred. I had to save myself from my thoughts, my shame. I had been so thirsty, so desperate for your love, that I was blind until it was almost too late. I felt stupid and exposed. It took everything I had to leave you. What small amount of confidence I once had was now shriveled, inaccessible. I doubted myself and every choice, every decision. If I was to survive, I had to become a true unbeliever. I had to let go of everything that had become familiar. To survive, I would have to change everything.

A year later, I was dating the man I would marry, my first husband. After several years of observing my constant chaos, after seeing the terrible choices I made, my friend David introduced us. He had gone to high school with Chris and thought he was the perfect antidote to the danger and drama. David set us up on a blind date, and I couldn't stand Chris. The poor guy was terrified of me. It was painful to try to carry on a conversation with him. Chris was quiet and shy, even timid. He wasn't very exciting, but David continually reminded me that that was kind of the point. Eventually, as I got to know Chris, things got better. He was genuinely a nice guy. I graduated, got a job, and moved to Santa Fe, and he drove from Albuquerque on the weekends. Then, after a little less than a year, I lost that job, due to lack of experience, according to my boss, who lived in Houston, and whom I had met three times. She never told me what I did wrong.

Jobless, I moved back to Albuquerque, and we got a place together. He was an introvert, and it was hard to get him to make decisions. He preferred taking a secondary role, which let me somewhat be in control, and that felt good most of the time. My friends constantly questioned why I was with him. They saw him as dull and me as a firecracker. It couldn't possibly work out. I could not articulate it at the time, but I knew Chris would not hurt me. He would not abandon me. He was safe. It was the late 80s and I couldn't find a job better than waitressing. We packed up and moved to Minnesota.

FIX

A position verified by reference to bearings taken off
a known point
such as a conspicuous landmark.

Getaway Car

The clock radio alarm went off, and I reached over to smack it, to stop the whiny, electronic bleating. I had been staring and blinking at the ceiling in my childhood bedroom for hours. I was thinking about the room, with its many personalities and versions, and what happened here, over the years. The pink and white striped wallpaper, and jumble of stuffed animals. All the times my grandfather, John, visited from Colorado, and found me in my hiding places, tracking me by the scent of my fear, like a bear, like a wolverine, while my parents were at work. The smell of his red packets of Prince Albert pipe tobacco. His plaid shirts. His false teeth. The Listerine on his breath.

I thought about the hours I spent practicing the flute, the French horn, speeches, and running play lines in my room. The AC/DC and Judas Priest and Bruce Springsteen posters. The Brazilian exchange student I kissed on this bed when I was 17. I had left home more than six years earlier, and the room now smelled vaguely like my mother, like Clinique Happy perfume, stale smoke, and dusty costume jewelry.

This was it. I was getting married. My groom was currently a mile away, sleeping on a twin bed in my grandmother's basement. We had been living together for two years, but for some reason, maybe small town, maybe Catholic, we spent our last night of freedom apart. Freedom. I tried not to think about that.

It was time to get up, shower, and prepare for a very long day. I lay there for a few more minutes, practicing the smile I would use later. Later as in, Catholic church wedding. Riding around town in the antique trolley my father had rented. A reception at the local Elk's Lodge, with its tiki torches, brown carpet, and drink tickets. It was my wedding day, planned by our mothers and grandmothers and my father. Though, to be fair, several months earlier, my father had offered us $5,000 to elope. I still don't know if he was serious. We probably should have taken the money.

As I got ready to pitch myself out of bed, I heard my father's clock radio switch on, on the other side of the wall. Growing up, during the week it was always Paul Harvey and the news of the day. That morning, an October Saturday, it was the muffled sound of Air Supply and a droning local DJ. Sometimes, my father would light a cigarette first thing, but on this day, the day his only daughter was getting married, he was all business. His feet hit the floor, and before I knew it, he was in the shared family bathroom, door closing with a chunk. It was at that moment that I lost my mind.

I leapt out of bed, yanked open my bedroom door, and yelled at the bathroom door, "I NEED TO TAKE A SHOWER! IT'S MY TURN!" After my father hollered that I could just wait a few minutes, I became enraged. An emotional fuse had been lit. I shut my bedroom door, pulled on some clothes, and stalked out into the kitchen. Before anyone could ask me what I was doing, I grabbed my keys and my purse, pulled open the back door, slammed it closed and headed for the driveway, where my white car was parked. I hopped in, started it up and backed out of the driveway and onto the street, fast. I may have done a smokey burnout in the street, or maybe not. I had no destination in mind, I just knew I had to get the hell out of that house. I was suffocating.

    I drove around my small hometown, up one street and down another. I finally ended up at the park down by the river. The Mississippi had been a constant in my childhood and young adulthood. As a little girl, I had spent hours sitting on the levee fishing with my "good" grandfather, Carl, and far more sunbathing, while my father piloted our small boat, and my mother smoked Benson & Hedges and waved at fellow boaters. Sunday summer afternoons were spent anchored by the dam, fishing, getting a tan and eating tuna sandwiches or fried chicken. It was one place where I felt closest to being at peace.

    That October Saturday, I sat in my car and just watched the current flow, admiring the gorgeous fall colors of the sugar maples and birches. I thought about not going back to the house. Maybe ever. It was 1990, before wireless technology. Before pagers. I was anonymous, I was untethered. I thought about going back to Ireland, where I did my semester abroad and met a boy. Not the boy I was marrying. I thought about moving to New York. I thought a lot of things. Then, mostly I thought about how disappointed my grandmothers were going to be if I didn't show up to the church in my white dress and veil. I was the oldest granddaughter on one side, and the youngest on the other. I pictured my father explaining to 150 people that there was not going to be a wedding. How very angry he would be. How embarrassed he would be, getting ribbed by his buddies at the Elk's Lodge for months, years, to come. I pictured my mother crying, wailing how I had ruined her day, the day she had put so much effort into. I finally got around to thinking about my groom. I guessed he would be disappointed, too. Probably.

In the protection of my getaway car, I hid for more than an hour, away from everyone more excited about the wedding than I was. Decisions had to be made. I set aside the weight, the peculiar tightness in my chest. The anxiety an animal feels as the door to the cage clanks shut. Domestication is inevitable. I put the car in gear and slowly drove back to my parents' house. "Where the hell have you been? We were going to send out a search party," my father demanded, as I walked into the kitchen. "I need to take a shower," I said. "I'm getting married."

For the rest of the day, I plastered on what I thought was an approximation of a young woman who was excited on her wedding day, maybe even a little giddy. She smiled and said all the right things. She looked like me, but she was not me, she was an imposter, playing the part of the happy bride.

That caged feeling, the chafing against expectations and obligations never truly went away. Chris was fine with whatever I wanted to do, so it wasn't necessarily about him, though he always felt a little clingy, a little dependent. He had never lived on his own. He had left his parents' house to move in with me. He was still in college, at the University of Minnesota, trying to get his bachelor's degree, and working evenings at a sporting goods store. My healing journey was not smooth, not continuous, and not without conflicts, both internal and external. Examining them later, I was struggling with the opposing feelings of craving freedom and wanting protection and safety. I tried my best to ignore them both. We bought a house, and we had a baby. Those feelings did not go away.

EPHEMERALS

Ephemeral maps: Snapshots in time that provide a contemporary view of a situation.

The Rites of Spring

It was Easter and the tablecloth was on fire. We were gathered at the table in the good dining room and had made an effort to look nice and get along as best we could, given the years-long tension between my father and uncle. There was history. My uncle thought my father was an uneducated brute, yet was jealous of his recent business success. My father thought my uncle was a free-loading fake, with his too-white capped teeth and name-dropping, who never disciplined his children. My mother and aunt stayed out of it, at least in public. Shortly after we sat down, my father at the head of the table, my cheerful German grandfather, Carl at the foot, grace was said, and it was clear that my mother was sinking under the heavy burden of cheap scotch, gulps stolen in the basement when she told us, *I have to check on something.*

The long dining table was loaded with food, a white platter groaning with pink salty ham slices, small bowls of green and black olives, a basket of warm brown 'n serve rolls, and the weird "healthy" salad my aunt always insisted on bringing. My mother smoked while the rest of us passed the bowls and baskets, salt and pepper shakers, and the flowered butter dish. The end of her cigarette grew long until the ashy worm broke off and plopped on the light blue lace tablecloth. Soon after, the weight of that white cigarette, glowing orange on one end with coral lipstick on the other, became too much for her drooping hand, and it went into freefall, cartwheeling to the tablecloth in slow motion, a single rotation. It came to rest next to her water glass.

At first, no one noticed but me. I made it my job to notice things. My tough little Irish grandmother was complaining about people who only attended Mass on Christmas and Easter, and sat in "her" pew. My brother and cousins chattered and compared the Matchbox cars they found in their Easter baskets. My uncle was ranting about the shortcomings in the moral character of the latest parolee added to his caseload, and excitedly telling us about the next sportscar he was going to buy, despite his civil servant salary and mountain of debt. Every year or two, he turned up in a different car for us to admire. Fawn over. A Karmann Ghia, an MG, a vintage Mercedes. My aunt, as usual, was quiet during his tirade. So was I.

The end of my mother's cigarette blossomed a perfect hole where it dropped, first eating the lacy fabric, then melting the vinyl table pad underneath. We could smell the chemical reaction of foam turning to liquid. My mother slowly lifted her head and tried to focus. My father stood up, clattering the good silverware against his plate, and then everything happened fast. He grabbed the glass water pitcher and sloshed enough ice water to extinguish the tiny flame that had sprouted in front of my mother. As he set the pitcher down, the handle bumped the glass candleholder in front of him, and toppled the white taper to the tablecloth, igniting the space next to the bowl of scalloped potatoes with real flames. Swearing, he splashed more water across the table, and set the pitcher down on the spongy tablecloth, while the dining room filled with the unpleasant smell of burned vinyl mingled with the scent of asparagus. Red-faced, from someplace deep inside his chest my father found the words and roared at my mother, "Get the hell out of here, go to bed!" She got up slowly, like she was reconnecting all of her parts, and lurched down the hall toward the bedroom, mumbling.

No one spoke. The ham with its sticky rings of canned pineapple and stakes of cloves had been forgotten, and the asparagus cooled in its buttery pool. My aunt had stopped taking small bites of food and was twisting her jade bracelet. Before that day, my mother had worked hard to pace herself at family events and was somewhat successful in masking how bad the drinking had gotten. My aunt asked quietly, brown eyes focused on the table, "Should we do something? Should we call someone? She really needs help."

Across the table, my grandmother tossed her blue cloth napkin to cover the mess on the table, and said tightly, "All's well that ends well," and asked my uncle to pass the Jell-O salad. I could feel my face and neck start to blotch, my emotional early warning system, and I focused hard on the porcelain owls in the China cabinet. I was not allowed to cry at the table.

I recalled that Easter, twenty years later, in my early

thirties and a mother myself, when we staged the intervention. It took weeks of planning. I argued incessantly with the insurance company, researched local treatment programs, talked to facilitators, and decided who would attend, and what we would say. We would hold the intervention in the living room of the house I grew up in. We had our assigned seats: loveseat, white chair, dining room chair, and the other white chair. My mother's chair stood apart.

In quiet moments, I considered, with no small amount of fear, that this would fray the last thread of my relationship with my mother. She had birthed me, and we loved each other, either by choice or obligation. I'm not sure which. She was so very sick. I hungered to be close to her, and for her to be able to be close to me, too, but maybe that was a fool's errand. After the intervention, what if the door closed, and we would just be done with one another? It was worth the price to save her, or at least that's what I thought all those years ago.

That Friday morning, I woke up early and thought about what would happen, or at least what was supposed to happen. I got in my car and drove the hour to my parents' house. I was so distracted and jittery that I barely paid attention. When I arrived mid-morning, the house was dark. I flipped on the kitchen lights and walked down the hallway toward my father's bedroom.

My father was in his bedroom with the door closed, and my mother was still asleep, in hers. I found my father sitting slump-shouldered on the side of his bed, oxygen cranked up, TV on. He had told me days before that with his end-stage COPD, the intervention would be too much for him. He would not be attending. Looking back, I think he was just scared of what my mother would do to him when she came home from treatment if she thought he had anything to do with sending her away. She was drinking all the time by then and was getting physically violent. She had even thrown a skillet at his head during an argument. My father put a lock on his office door both to keep her out and safely store his firearms. It was awful seeing him have to take such measures to avoid my mother.

My heart broke a bit every time I saw my strong, confident, resourceful and capable father tethered to a slim hose, two little nose cannulas delivering oxygen to his scarred lungs, his mobility slowed to a shuffle. When I saw my mother, drunk, reeking of cheap scotch, eyes bloodshot, slurring her words, I could feel nothing but contempt. I knew in my head that she had a disease – they both did, but I could not dig deep and experience feelings of love, or empathy for my mother. At the time, that didn't bother me. For my parents, this was the pledge of for better or worse, in sickness and health at its worst and most hypocritical. Neither could take care of the other.

I left my father in his room and closed his door. I paced the light blue carpet down the hall and into the living room. Eventually, the others arrived for the intervention. There were six of us. The interventionist was the last to arrive, thirty minutes late. He showed up in a rumpled short-sleeved shirt and brown tie, exuding arrogance and a frowning type of scorn. We had been worried about the element of surprise, but my mother was still sleeping the sleep of the dead.

My mother's friend, Vicky, and I woke my mother up and brought her to the living room. As instructed, we marched through all the intervention steps: we read the impact statements and the heartfelt letters we had spent hours writing and rewriting, stopping just short of outright pleading with her. We all cried, except my uncle and the interventionist, and we could not stop. We clutched tissues, shredding them as we spoke. The crying came from a deep place of hurt, relief, fear, and the promise of optimism. Maybe she could finally be a healthy, functioning grandmother to my son. Maybe the intervention could work. Maybe she would see so many people still loved her, and find the willpower to quit drinking. Maybe she could finally help take care of my father. We all wanted her to quit drinking. That day, we thought willpower was all it took. We were so naïve.

The interventionist, a social worker, a professional who dealt in the currency of pain and billable hours, and my uncle were friends. The men spent much of the costly session exchanging told-you-so looks and side-barring snarky commentary. The rest of us sat, silently awaiting instructions, while they had their little conversations we could barely hear.

The intervention was nothing like what you see on television. In the real world, you sit in your parents' living room, not some sterile studio, and you smell musky sweat and unwashed hair, combined with the unmistakable sharpness of scotch leaching from pores. You smell the rank, acidic breath from unbrushed teeth and a fuzzy tongue. You observe wet, bloodshot eyes, struggling to stay open. In the real world, she is still drunk, very drunk, from the night before. In the real world, your ears ring from her screaming - how we were all traitors who didn't give a shit about her. That we should just leave her alone. That we should get the hell out of her house. In the real world, she doesn't sit quietly and stare at her lap while we share our feelings and emotions, reading from pieces of paper damp with the sweat of our palms. In the real world, there is her unleashed rage. My uncle and I got the worst of it. He was nonchalant, neutral, and even smirked a few times.

I was trying to hold all my pieces together, as she kept blasting away. I was sweating. We were all sweating. We tried every tactic we could think of and asked my mother over and over if she would agree to go to treatment, just like the interventionist had told us to. For the most part, he just sat and watched our loud and soggy process, as we kept lobbing our requests at my mother, and she fired back with vitriol and increasing desperation. In that room, we were surrounded by family photos from happier times, or at least when we were better at faking it. Our younger selves looked on, as the room pulsed with frustration and anguish.

Eventually, my mother minimally agreed to go to treatment, by which I mean she stopped screaming no. We were all exhausted. We all felt raw and unprotected, except for my uncle, her only sibling, who looked triumphant and satisfied. And the interventionist, who kept checking his watch, was eager to present his invoice and get on with his day.

Vicky and I got my mother out of her stained pajamas and into jeans and a sweatshirt and tried to brush her hair. My mother stalled when we tried to help her with her shoes, flexing her feet, and refusing to put them on. We grabbed the duffle bag we had prepacked with a few of her things and got her out the door and into my father's white Cadillac for the 60-minute drive to the hospital in Minneapolis. I was the driver. I had suggested to my father that she attend the local hospital's treatment program. It was 15 minutes away, and it was where he had spent what he called his 28-day vacation getting sober (but not staying sober) years earlier. He said my mother would never agree to a program where she might see someone she knew. It was a strange time to be considering the optics.

My mother sat in the backseat of the car, wedged between two of her few remaining friends, Vicky and Jo. We kept her away from the door handles and potential escape. My mother was crying, really wailing, at first. Then, likely because she could not garner enough attention and sympathy, she switched tactics became enraged, and began to fire a vicious barrage of insults at me from the backseat. I kept driving down the highway, knuckles white on the steering wheel, jaw tight. I loosely knew where I was going, as my father had mapped out the journey on Map Quest for me. The streets widened to highways, and highways widened to freeways. We drove past cornfields, carpeted with green life, and we could hear crows squabbling, as they perched on long drooping powerlines. A black dog barked from the gravel driveway of a farm, at first menacing, then sounding lonely.

My mother's friends murmured consolation and reassurance and offered to pray the rosary with her. I turned the radio on and tuned it to the pop-rock station my mother liked. I needed a distraction from the coiled anticipation in the car, the crooning of these women who completely underestimated my mother, and the anxiety of knowing that something or someone was going to blow. As we edged closer to the city, we passed fast food joints, used car dealerships, and local bars, their parking lots filled with cars and trucks, even though it was barely past noon on a weekday. Billboards for plumbers and realtors guarded the freeway and as we passed the airport, there were white Northwest Airlines jets on the tarmac, ready to go anywhere but here. My mother had grown quiet in the backseat, and I thought she may have been asleep. In truth, she was getting her second wind.

We were getting close. As I began to look for the freeway exit to the hospital, I made the terrible mistake of announcing it would only be a few more minutes. My mother came to life. She became unhinged. She started clumsily kicking the back of my seat, grabbing at my hair. Her friends, caught off-guard, tried to capture her hands, but she was fast, and determined. My mother once again loudly bombarded me with sloppy words, the tinge of slurring doing nothing to diminish the most hurtful things she could think of. She bellowed that I was ungrateful and selfish, a terrible daughter, and she hoped I would have children who hated me as much as I obviously hated her. She weaponized my secrets, as her friends learned of my past eating disorder and my anxiety. My weaknesses. The closer we got to the hospital, the closer I got to throwing up. I kept reminding myself to stop holding my breath.

Several times my mother screamed that I was a coward, which was the opposite of the truth. I focused on the road. My face turned red, blotched. I did not cry.

As I reflect on that day, I think about how much I wanted to save my mother, in juxtaposition to how little love I felt for her. I was incredibly angry that she could not, did not want to save herself. It brought up all those feelings again of not being protected by her when I was a child. And here I was, trying to protect her, trying to keep her from drinking herself to death. I felt deeply resentful, but my overwhelming sense of responsibility, to please, to fix, drowned out the resentment, at least temporarily.

A few years before the intervention I had "divorced" my mother for an entire year, when my son was a baby. During a visit to our house, my mother was holding the baby and was so drunk she didn't notice him slipping out of her arms and falling toward the floor. When the rest of us sprang into action, she was completely oblivious to what she had done. That was the last straw for me. My therapist and I agreed I would have no contact with her while trying to get some distance and perspective. To heal, if that was possible. It also provided an opportunity for her to choose to get help with her alcoholism. I was clear that if she did so, she was welcome to see her grandson. But, if nothing changed, which it didn't, I was determined to save my child and protect him, unlike what I had experienced. That was not negotiable.

My father was frustrated during the "divorce," insisting I had put him in a terrible position, as he and my brother were allowed to see my son, but my mother was not. He told me I was being selfish. That I was making things impossible for him at home. Once, he even accused me of being on a power trip. I think he was desperate to make everything okay, which was my goal, too. We just had different ways of going about it. I was slowly starting to realize through the gift of therapy, that maybe not everything was my fault, and just maybe I could expect that others would claim responsibility for their actions. I didn't hold tightly to that expectation, though, because history had taught me otherwise. But I could feel an infinitesimal shift in my thinking.

The Ambulance

The house was thick with tension. My seven-year-old daughter, Sarah, had been agitated and difficult all day. It felt like walking in the dark, and guessing where the tripwire might be. When asked to do something like, "Go wash your hands for lunch," she would immediately escalate into screaming in the highest and loudest pitch she had, "NO NO NO NO!" She would stomp to her room and slam the door as hard as she could. Then followed the loud thud and whomp of toys and books hitting her bedroom wall. It was exhausting. For all of us.

Independence Day weekend, 2003. It started like any other hot Midwestern, morning. The cicadas droned their joyful summer song at full volume into the humid air. It was the kind of day we longed for during dark January. I was cutting watermelon for a potluck the next day. The watermelon was heavy and particularly juicy, and the sticky pink liquid steadily trickled off the side of the white cutting board, and onto the dark gray countertop.

We were so happy and hopeful when Sarah joined our family at the age of three-and-a-half, in the summer of 1999. We were her twelfth foster care placement in less than two years, if you counted all the times she ping-ponged to and from her grandmother's house (29-day emergency placements – she refused to get her foster care license) to other relatives, and back to foster care. We met Sarah just a few times, had one overnight visit, and signed a six-month foster-adopt arrangement with the county. At the end of that time, we had to decide whether to adopt her or return her to the foster care system. Things did not go smoothly, but we toughed it out. Sarah was angry and physically violent and had many behaviors unfamiliar to us, like food hoarding. At the end of the six months, we could not stomach sending that little girl back into the swamp of foster care. We saw signs that terrible things may have happened to her in foster care, or at one of her relatives' homes, and we would not risk sending her back to that. We adopted her in December 1999, on the last day of the sixth month. We figured that with time, love and stability, the situation would improve. Her social worker kept telling us, "If you just love her enough, it's all going to be okay." We believed her. It was just one of the many lies told about broken children.

Instead, it got much worse. Sarah had an extreme form of attachment disorder, and the more we tried to get close to her and love her, the more she acted out. The pressure on her to love and trust must have felt terrifying, and she showed us the only ways she could – with her fists, her feet, her shrill screaming. She stole from other kids' lunches at her Catholic school, and from the teacher's desk. After kindergarten and then first grade, we were asked not to bring her back to the school. She lacked the cause-and-effect thinking other kids her age had. She would do things like slink behind her big brother, smack him in the head, walk over to me, with a concerned look, and say "Brother's crying."

Sarah had a laundry list of acronym-ed diagnoses, and it seemed like another one was added every month. I had spent hundreds of hours researching on the bourgeoning internet, and joined every online support group and listserve that could possibly help me figure out how to help this little girl. We brought her to every type of specialist we could find – pediatrician, psychologist, psychiatrist, therapist, attachment clinic, physical and occupational therapists. The state covered some of her medical costs, as did insurance, but every month, there were still big medical bills, which we could barely afford. Call it commitment, or stubbornness, or maybe I was just determined to try to fix her because I couldn't fix what I experienced as a child. I was not going to give up on her. Every time we called our social worker with another crisis, her refrain was that "there was no shame in disrupting the adoption and giving Sarah back to the county foster care system. Even though you are trying very hard, these things happen." Not in our family. I was determined.

That summer day, when I was cutting the watermelon, Sarah was in what my grandmother would have called, a mood. She leaned on me like a cat, bumping into me, over and over, trying to get attention. My repeated replies of, *in a minute, wait 'til I'm done with this, hold on a sec,* made her even more irritated. Then she asked for candy. She demanded it. Over and over. Sarah was obsessed with candy. From the early days after she joined our family, I found candy, granola bar, protein bar, and fruit snack wrappers under her bed and in her sheets. She snuck out of her room at night and roamed the house in search of treats. It didn't matter where I hid them, she found them, even if she had to stand on the kitchen counters. We were told in the minimal information we received from the social worker that Sarah "really liked candy." The truth was, in her nearly dozen foster care placements, candy had been used to motivate her, placate her, feed her, bribe her, calm her, reward her. Sweets had become another parent to her. We lived with those consequences.

  I continued cutting the melon, but her requests intensified into screeching, "I want candy NOWWW!" Then we reached the point where her love of candy and her hatred of being told no collided. She was screaming at me so loudly and intensely that her face was nearly purple, and the veins in her little neck stood out. As I turned to get a bowl, Sarah grabbed the knife off the cutting board. I turned back to face her, and before I could say anything, she shoved the knife at me. The end of the knife blade poked into my right thigh. If she had been taller and more accurate, the outcome would have been grave. I didn't know if it was luck, divine intervention, or just quick reflexes that kept the damage to a minimum. None of that changed the fact that my seven-year-old daughter had just stabbed me with a very sharp knife.

  Once my brain and body reconnected after the shock, I grabbed the knife from her and threw it in the sink. Sarah was so out of control I don't know if she was even aware of what was happening. She was prone to massive tantrums lasting one, two, or even four hours. She screamed obscenities at us, cried, kicked her bedroom and closet doors, and had driven a grapefruit-sized hole in the pink wall of her room by laying on her bed and drilling the wall with the heels of her shoes. This time, though, this was not like any other meltdown. There was a hum on a brand-new frequency, like a drone, seeking a place to land.

I grabbed both of Sarah's wrists and held tight. I wrapped her in a bear hug, lifted her the few steps to the hallway, and pulled her down with me to the carpeted floor. Her shrieks were piercing and my ears were clanging. Sarah tried to bite me. She tried to kick me and yank my fingers. I was stunned, I was angry, but most of all I was just scared. How could my child be capable of doing something like this?

I held Sarah down, both of us sweating, red-faced. I held her wrists with my hands, her motoring legs under my calves. She raged and cried and screamed. The sounds coming out of her were otherworldly, guttural, animal-like. I must have been screaming too, but I don't remember what I said. We stayed like that for what felt like hours, locked in our hallway battle, but it was probably more like 10 or 15 minutes. Eventually, my ex-husband, Chris came up from the basement after he heard all the ruckus. I yelled to him "Sarah stabbed me with a knife! Dr. Hosfield said that if we couldn't calm her down, to call 911, and have her taken to Abbott!" Abbott Northwestern was the only hospital in the Twin Cities metro area with a pediatric mental health unit and the only place that could meet her needs. My legs and arms were starting to shake from effort, and panic was rising like a snake squeezing my insides. I knew I could not contain her much longer.

Chris stared at the scene. He did not move. "Get the phone godammit!" He remained frozen in his spot just outside the kitchen. I don't think he could process the chaos. I jumped off Sarah and grabbed the black cordless phone off the counter. I dropped back down to the floor and tried to restrain Sarah as best I could with one arm. She continued to scream. I dialed 911. "What is your emergency?" the operator asked. "My seven-year-old daughter stabbed me with a knife, we can't get her to calm down! I need an ambulance! She needs an ambulance!" She has mental issues! She takes medication! We need help!" I may have said she tried to murder me. I may have said she was dangerous. I tried to remember the language Dr. Hosfield told me to use, but I couldn't access anything besides what was in front of me. The operator asked who was screaming, and I said it was Sarah. She asked if I was injured, and I said, "I don't know, I think so." She said she would dispatch an ambulance, and told me to make sure the front door was unlocked. I yelled to Chris, and he finally re-animated and went down the stairs and unlocked the door. I think I stayed on the phone with the dispatcher.

A few minutes later, I heard the mechanical wail of a police siren approaching our house. The officer parked the squad car at the curb in front of the house walked up to the front door and knocked loudly. Chris let him in and led the officer up the stairs to the main level. The officer assessed the scene. Watermelon, half sliced on the white cutting board, juice dripping on the floor. A young girl screaming in a voice that was hoarse and jagged. A blonde woman in shorts and a t-shirt on hands and knees in the hallway, restraining the girl with her body and telling her something (indistinguishable). The discarded cordless phone, lying in the hallway. Drops of blood on the white carpet.

The officer stood in the kitchen and asked me what happened. I started to answer him, but he couldn't hear me over the sound of Sarah's continued protestations. The officer approached us, and Sarah got even more upset, wild-eyed, and once again started kicking at me and thrashing on the floor. I stayed where I was, blurting out answers, until Sarah finally started slowing, calming, the barrage of noise now grunts, and what sounded like hissing. Chris switched places with me, the crisis on the downswing. I got up, sweaty, shaky, dizzy, spent. The officer wanted to see my injury. I had been running on 100% adrenaline, so I had no idea how bad the wound was, or what it looked like. My leg was bleeding, a steady trickle. The officer got a paper towel and told me to hold that on the wound. At least, that's how I remember it.

We heard another shrieking siren coming down our street.

The ambulance arrived. An EMT got out and headed toward our front door, bag in hand. He announced himself at the open door, came in, and briefly conferred with the officer. As they spoke, they glanced at Sarah and me several times. Chris released Sarah's wrists as she wound down, snuffling, wiping her nose with the back of her hand. He unfolded from his position on the floor. For the first time in what seemed like hours, Sarah was completely unrestrained and she sat up. There was an absence of sound. It was over. She was safe. We all were safe. We had survived. The EMT asked Sarah to sit on a chair. Surprisingly she did. She looked at him curiously. The EMT took her pulse and blood pressure and told her she did a great job. He looked at Chris and me, frowned and said her blood pressure and her pulse were extremely high. He took her temperature in her ear, at which point Sarah started wiggling, but she was able to sit long enough to get a reading. The EMT said that was elevated as well. He asked if Sarah was taking any medications, and I said, "Quite a few." He asked what health conditions she had.

We kept a thick blue folder on the kitchen island that contained her medical information. I grabbed it and held it out to him. It listed all of Sarah's health and mental health providers, including Dr. Hosfield, Sarah's pediatric psychiatrist.

I rattled off the list of Sarah's mental health issues, the acronyms rolling off my tongue like I was reciting countries and capitals. RAD – reactive attachment disorder, GAD – generalized anxiety disorder, ADD– attention deficit disorder, IED – intermittent explosive disorder, FAS– fetal alcohol syndrome/

rule out, ODD – oppositional defiant disorder, SPD – sensory processing disorder, pediatric depression, prenatal drug exposure to meth, marijuana. I told him to look on the meds page in the folder for her current meds and dosages. We had tried so many over the years, I didn't trust myself to give him the right details. Gabapentin. Geodon. Depakote. Risperdal. Seroquel. Klonopin. Remeron.

    The EMT finished examining Sarah. He received a garbled communication on the radio perched on his shoulder. They had been cleared to transport Sarah to Abbott Hospital. Then, as an afterthought, he asked to see my injury. I showed him my leg and noticed that at some point I had dropped the paper towel. He said, "It doesn't look real bad," and I would probably not need stitches. He went to his bag, pulled out a large square bandage, and affixed it to my thigh.

    Chris signed some paperwork for the officer and the EMT. The police officer kept glancing at me, and his crumpled brow telegraphed his suspicion around the day's events. How could I possibly send him a look that said, "I am trying to save this child." I hoped we never saw him again. I volunteered to go with Sarah in the ambulance. I grabbed the blue folder. I went to my red purse and pulled out my driver's license and insurance card because the EMT said I would need them. I put them in the pocket of my shorts. Chris said he would stay home and wait for our nine-year-old son, Samson to come home from playing video games with his friend down the street.

Paperwork signed, decisions made, the EMT asked Sarah if she could walk to the ambulance. She followed the EMT down the driveway and I followed her, all of us squinting in the blinding sunshine. When we reached the ambulance, a second EMT lifted Sarah into the back of the ambulance, sat her on the gurney, then asked her to lie down. She followed his commands without complaint. I stepped up into the ambulance and sat where the EMT told me. The driver slammed one door and then the other. He started the engine and pulled out of our driveway. The two windows in the back of the ambulance were small and square, providing a portal to the calm sunshiny outside world. Our house got smaller and smaller, and the canopy of tall trees waved in the breeze, saluting us.

I had never ridden in an ambulance before, or I didn't remember if I did. I focused on the view through the back windows for the entire ride. Looking through those windows reminded me of when I was a kid, and sat in the "way back" of the station wagon. I watched as life for other people, outside the ambulance, went on. Drivers in cars on the freeway, some smoking, some laughing, some drinking a soda out of a McDonald's cup. When we turned off the freeway and stopped at a red light, I saw a couple standing on a corner, arguing and shaking their fists. I couldn't hear what they were saying. On the sidewalk near the hospital, an older man in denim short shorts walked his tiny brown dog on a red leash.

With no sirens blaring, it took us about 25 minutes to

get to the hospital. I barely registered the EMT talking to Sarah, checking her blood pressure, the various beeps, the lines and numbers, and the squiggles on the machine screens. I thought again and again about what happened and wondered how we got there. Got here.

We arrived at the ER as the sunlight was melting from white into the soft yellow of late afternoon. Sliding into the cement belly of the hospital should have felt good. I should have felt relief that we would get help, and the experts would take over. But I felt wary and anxious. Would the doctors and nurses look at me like that police officer did? Was this my fault?

Sarah was wheeled into the ER, me trailing behind her, and transferred to a bed. The curtain was pulled and wrapped around to create a small room-like area. The doctors and nurses whirled in and out, leaving the curtain flapping in their wake. As I sat, I held the blue folder to my chest like a talisman. I opened it several times to give the doctors and nurses Sarah's current meds and her diagnoses. Sarah's blood pressure and temperature were checked. I gave consent. At some point, a nurse affixed a white wristband to Sarah's arm. Sarah said she was hungry, so a nurse brought her some graham crackers and Jell-O. Sarah seemed to relax, her eyes puffy from crying. Every time a doctor or nurse, or med student pulled the curtain aside and walked in, I asked if Sarah was going to be admitted. No one had an answer. Hours went by.

Outside the thin shield of curtain, we heard yelling and

crying, the clattering of gurneys traversing the ER, urgent medical voices. The Fourth of July weekend was in full swing. Finally, a nurse stuck her head around the curtain and said that Sarah would be admitted, at least for observation. We were assured, over and over, that someone would come very soon to take us to the pediatric mental health unit. Finally, an orderly arrived with a wheelchair, and we headed toward the elevator.

When we arrived at the mental health unit, I was not prepared. I was not ready to see the scuffed cream-colored double locked doors, the entrance devoid of color, of life. There was a call box on the wall next to the doors, to gain access to the unit, like a secret city. Once the orderly announced himself and Sarah, the lock on the doors buzzed and clicked. We could enter. I had been told this was a highly staffed unit, and the patients were constantly monitored and supervised. When we entered, I saw a girl about Sarah's age wandering down the hall, alone, with no staff in sight.

A nurse took Sarah to weigh her, get her vitals, find her pajamas, and help her get settled in her room. In the meantime, I sat on a tan vinyl chair in front of the nurses' station, unmoving. Another nurse asked me if I wanted something to eat or drink while I waited, and told me there were vending machines downstairs. That's when I realized that I hadn't brought my purse. I had nothing but my ID and insurance card. The nurse kindly went into a storage area, unlocked a cabinet, and came back with a warm can of 7-Up and some pretzels.

By the time I went in to tell Sarah goodnight, it was late, maybe 10:30 pm. She told me goodbye with a stiff hug and little emotion. The day's battle had left me dazed, and I was trying not to cry. Despite everything that happened, I didn't want to leave Sarah there, alone. I didn't want her to be afraid. I didn't want her to feel like I'd given up on her, abandoned her. I knew how that felt.

I walked back to the nurse's station and asked to use the phone to call Chris, to tell him I was ready to be picked up at the hospital. He answered and said our son, Samson, was sleeping, and he didn't want to wake him up. He would not be coming to get me.

After I hung up, I felt a sickening wave of alarm, as I realized I had no car, no phone, no purse, and no money. The nurse at the station must have seen my face or heard my side of the conversation. I asked her what I should do. Sympathetic, she reached into a locked drawer under the desk and pulled out a green slip of paper. She told me it was a taxi voucher. They had them available for patients or visitors who were indigent or could not afford transportation. She called the taxi service to arrange a pickup for me and handed me the voucher. I thanked her. I felt deeply ashamed. I took the elevator to the main floor and walked to the entrance of the hospital. I waited for the taxi in the warm semi-darkness of that July night and watched the moths gather and flood the streetlights.

When the taxi arrived, I climbed into the back seat and gave my address. As we drove, night air and the city smells washed over me, and I thought how different this ride was from the one seven hours earlier. They were also strangely alike. My questions were not answered, problems were not solved. They were just deferred for however long Sarah would be in the hospital. Sarah was so broken by the trauma in her young life, by the people who abused her, who let her down, who put her in danger. For the first time in the four years since we had adopted her, I could not see a path forward, a way to help her heal. The thing that felt most like hope had dissolved.

We drove west on I-94, out to the suburbs. I thought about how I didn't have any money to tip the taxi driver. I didn't have a key to get in the house. I didn't know how I could walk down that hallway next to the kitchen.

But then, words coalesced in my head. They were pulled from a place, a time more than twenty-five years earlier. They felt urgent.

Don't give up on her. Save her.

The words came as I remembered how I felt at her age, at seven years old. Frightened. Confused. Distrustful. Unprotected. Unsafe. No one had paid attention to what was happening. No one had reached out to help me. To save me. I was alone.

The taxi pulled into the driveway. I was home. The lights were off and the door was locked.

Fifteen months later, Chris and I divorced, and our family fractured and divided in half. It didn't get any easier.

Malibu

My brother, Tim, and I rented a luxury car at LAX. Maybe an Infiniti, maybe a Mercedes. Not for the status, well, maybe for the status, but mostly because it reminded us of family, of the road, of the need to drive that bubbled in our veins. That is what we did, in my family, when we didn't know what else to do. And this was a time when we did not know what else to do. Tim and I had flown to California to spend four days with my daughter, Sarah, but only saw her for a total of six excruciating hours. I should have known better because I had made this trip before. It's what mothers do. It's what I do. She knew we were coming. I don't know if that was good or bad.

The morning after we arrived, Tim and I walked out of the cool, marbled hotel lobby, and the brightness blasted us like a crisis, a burn that marked the end of optimism. My pupils constricted like the slamming of a door. I prayed for some muted light, relief, maybe a passing cumulus cloud. Even the blue of the sky was bleached. Los Angeles at the end of summer could be so cruel.

We drove the 20 minutes to Sarah's sober living house. There had been so many. She was sitting on the curb when we pulled up. She stumbled to the rental car – a husk on shaky legs. She curled up in the backseat like a snake that had lost its coil. Her unwashed hair, leggings coated with cat hair, and wrinkled tie-dyed t-shirt told a story that I didn't want to guess the ending of. Sarah was in her 20s but looked both much older and much younger.

We had hugged on the street in a brittle way, and the chemical longing between mother and child failed to find a reaction or ignite. The touch was brief and guarded - three pats on two backs. There was so much history, so much pain between us. Her struggles with relationships. With rules. Her love affairs and messy breakups with alcohol and drugs. Like an abused lover, she was lured back, over and over. It started with alcohol, then marijuana. Then, opioids became her solace, her best friend, her love. Until they weren't. For years, I had struggled to understand her, help her, love her, and she hated me back.

Because of her severe attachment disorder, the more I tried to flood her with my love, the worse it felt for her, and the harder she shoved back. We had a complicated relationship, Sarah and I, back when we had a relationship. But on that day, our relationship was only strung together by requests for money, and our health insurance, which had paid for all her stays in rehab, and a dozen sober living facilities. I don't think she understood, or maybe she didn't care, that our Blue Cross Blue Shield policy had paid out nearly $1,000,000 for her care over the years, much of it for chemical dependency treatment. We did not take her off the insurance, because without it, we didn't know what would happen to her. We were afraid for her. There had already been several stretches of a month or longer, where we didn't know where she was. If she was alive. Every time my phone rang after 8 pm, I was scared to answer. I kept my phone by the bed every single night. Waiting.

The heft of all the lies, half-truths, and promises sat between us now, a fourth passenger in the rental car. I asked her questions, and each response cracked into small words and smaller still, until there remained only jumbles of letters fluttering behind us on the freeway. Finally, we stopped talking altogether, leaving the rest unsaid.

Sarah slept, or pretended to between Woodland Hills and Malibu. I was glad we had found the correct sober living house. There had been so many late-night moves, with her belongings stuffed into black garbage bags, much like how she arrived at our house from foster care, as a toddler. Those garbage bags were white. I still have them. They contain the dirty clothes and a few broken toys she arrived with. Sarah had been at this particular sober house for weeks, after her fifth or sixth time in rehab. I had lost count. She had been in and out of treatment for five years, maybe six, since just after she barely graduated high school. After all the moves, anything she owned of value was long gone and any remnants of sentimentality were abandoned. We were heading to Malibu that day, not because of Sarah, but because Tim had never been there. Sarah said that she had been there a bunch of times before. She said a lot of things.

The sun blared like an angry god, and the tires felt like they were softening and hugging the hot roads. Ventura, Mulholland, the 101 laid before us like an invitation. We had reservations at the Paradise Cove Beach Café in Malibu. I chose it because it had good Yelp reviews. It was a Saturday and traffic crawled along the Pacific Coast Highway. It's not like the movies. Malibu was one long assault on the senses. The briny, bloated, fishy ocean smells blended with the AC blasting in the car. Families walked along the road, with overstuffed beach bags, chairs, and trucker hats. Tiny, colorful, expensive homes huddled together against the hoi polloi. Each home had a gate and a call box.

  Miraculously, Tim found a place to park at the restaurant. He eased into a spot next to a gleaming black Maybach and was impressed. We were early, so the three of us wandered out on the long pier behind the restaurant, suspended over the sparkling Pacific. We took selfies with our sunglasses on and showed all our teeth. We tilted our heads in a pantomime of joy at seeing one another.

  The restaurant was big and noisy. We were seated in a large red booth and we examined the huge laminated menu. Sarah ordered a fruity drink with an orchid in it, and a $29 plate of seafood spaghetti. When they arrived, she put the orchid behind her ear, smiled for a photo, sipped the drink, then slumped into the corner of the booth, and refused to eat or talk. I was confused by her behavior. I had never seen her like this, so aggressively disconnected, and I was concerned. Really concerned. It was clear that Sarah was very unwell. Every 15 minutes or so she sat up and slid out of the booth with a dramatic sigh, amid a loud jangle of keys, crystals, vape pen, and security alarm, all attached to the dirty lanyard around her neck. I could see her outside, vaping furiously and talking on the phone. She was vibrating with an energy I didn't recognize. My worry took up space in the booth. My lunch was congealing into a knot in my stomach. Tim and I finished our meal and had Sarah's boxed up.

On the freeway heading back to her sober house, she said the smell of the leftovers was making her sick. At first, she complained, then whined, and then she started to wail, inconsolable. She threatened to throw the food out the window because there was no place for us to pull over. She opened and closed her window in a nervy cadence. Finally, we exited the freeway and spotted a green trash can. We slid to the curb and dumped her meal.

I remember when she was in middle school, and we found out she was smoking weed with her friends, and getting drunk and throwing up in her dad's basement. Staying out late at night, with friends her dad didn't know. Sarah snuck her boyfriend in at night and sent him back out the window before her dad woke up. She lived with her dad because I had too many rules.

In ninth grade, she injured her knee in softball, and the doctor gave her OxyContin - with refills. In high school, she sold her Adderall pills to a Mexican girl gang, and we had to move her to another high school to avoid their violent wrath when she ran out of pills. I remember all the trips to the emergency room, starting when she was 15, with "11 on a scale of 10" stomach pain. She writhed in performative agony, sometimes right there, on the ghastly dirty hospital floor. At first, we blamed her endometriosis, which could be debilitatingly painful. She had several procedures to remove that endometrial tissue, and she was in less pain. For a while. The length of time when she felt okay, when she wasn't telling us that the pain was so terrible, that it kept her up all night, vomiting, grew shorter every year. Then shorter every few months. Only painkillers seemed to help her. Then, she started using fentanyl patches. That was frightening for us, but not for her. She said she had finally found the thing that "really worked" for her. She wanted, demanded, manipulated, and schemed for more. Always more.

  As she got older, her visits to various ERs around the Twin Cities got to be more frequent. And then, there were the other "episodes" that started not adding up. The time she ended up in her car on the side of the freeway, 20 miles from home, with no recollection of how she drove there. She started telling us that she was having times when she would "dissociate" and was not aware of what she was doing. There were car accidents, especially the last one, late at night, when she said she fell asleep at the wheel. She flipped into a ditch, and the car was nearly totaled. She walked away, unharmed, thankfully. She had either been using heroin or was in withdrawal.

Finally, she got fired from her nursing assistant job at the hospital, and would not tell us why. Looking back, she was likely not showing up for work, or stealing drugs. When she was 19 and 20, local ERs began to ban her, mark her as "drug-seeking" and turn her away.

Seeing her behave the way she was that day, in the backseat of the car, driving back from Malibu, her obvious discomfort, how irritable she was, took me back to those days. I felt so sad. For her. For me. I knew she had a disease, but I seemed to also forget. I felt used and angry. There was so little space left for empathy. I was exhausted and emotionally bankrupt. Her father was trying to pray her well. Nothing worked.

Every time she went to rehab, it was going to be different, she promised. We learned later that in some of the rehab facilities, and every one of the sober living houses, there were drugs. A lot of drugs. They could easily be purchased, or bartered. Every time she was in rehab or therapy, I pestered and begged her to invite me, or me and her father to family counseling. "We can figure this out," I said. Every time, her answer was, "It would just be too traumatizing for me. My therapist thinks it wouldn't be appropriate." I was pretty sure that was complete bullshit. I went to Nar-Anon meetings a few times. The other parents seemed as bewildered and angry as I was.

In LA, the night before we went to Malibu, she was a no-show for dinner, but later, she wanted Tim and I to pick her up and take her to Walmart. We rolled through cramped and filthy aisles in the store, and she tossed cans and boxes into the cart. We had picked a cart with a bad front wheel, and it made a dental grinding sound when she turned the corners. She casually mentioned that her food stamps had run out a week earlier, and she was eating whatever she could "borrow" from her housemate. He was charging her interest. I didn't know what that meant, or how she would pay. I focused on the cart and the bad wheel.

She gathered a dozen cups of yogurt, loaves of bread, peanut butter, and packages of cheese. Boxes of mac and cheese, pasta. She slid five packages of bacon into the cart. She didn't want eggs, but she needed five pounds of bacon. The questions tickled in my throat like the silk inside sweet corn. I wanted to ask. I didn't.

The floor in that Walmart was so dirty my sandals stuck to it, and made a thwick sound as we went down each row. The entire store smelled like overripe bananas and generic fabric softener. Every item more than ten dollars was locked in a glass case, even the hair conditioner she wanted.

As we drove her back to Woodland Hills, she couldn't remember how to get to her house, and then she couldn't remember the address. She was distressed and loud. She called one of her housemates, and we looked up the address on Google Maps. Sarah was quiet but agitated during the car ride. I could hear the soft sound of her heels pile-driving onto the floor of the back seat, and the return flip of her sandals. She only asked: "Do you think you can miss two periods because of stress?" We stopped at CVS and bought two pregnancy tests. I said, "You cannot have a baby right now." She didn't argue—at least not that day.

I helped her carry the twelve bags from Walmart up the steep stairs into her house. Tim waited in the car. Fourteen people were living in the five-bedroom house. As she opened the front door, we passed through a curtain of smells: dog, cat, unwashed sheets, stale coffee, cigarettes. The blinds were open, but it was murky despite the relative brightness of early evening. Dust motes danced in the shards of the sun. Most of her housemates were gone – either working or at NA or AA meetings.

She showed me her room. She seemed resigned, not proud. This was only the second of her sober living homes I had seen. I was shocked. Our insurance paid $5,000 a month, just for a space for her to sleep in a dirty, claustrophobic bedroom she shared with two other women. I did some quick math, and that was $70,000 being paid to the owners every month. The sober living home charged another $5,000 a month for ambiguous "services," like drug testing and transportation to support groups. The rickety metal bunkbeds took up most of the floor space in her room, and her clothes spilled out of a broken suitcase, like flour from a ripped bag. A black garbage bag poked out from under her bunk, she said that's where she kept the rest of her stuff. How could this place promote wellness, healing?

We put her groceries into locked cabinets and marked her

name on the cold stuff for the fridge with a Sharpie. Her hands were trembling like new leaves in the spring breeze. The unnamed thing that had been gnawing at me revealed itself. "Tell me. Are you using again?" She refused to look at me and shrugged her shoulders like she was trying to move the weight between us. She said, "Absolutely not." She said a lot of things. Later, she mentioned she may have gotten something from that guy at the beach, that one time. But only one time. She didn't have a job or money, so she paid with the only currency she had. I tried not to think about that. We restocked her housemate's shelf. I couldn't do anything about the interest he was charging her. I felt ineffective, out of my depth. I hugged her, both of us stiff, unyielding. I gave her fifty dollars and said goodbye.

    Now, with the gift of time and distance since that day, I see things more clearly. I was so angry at her and myself for thinking things would somehow be different. Most of all, I was furious at her disease, not understanding that I was seething at that motherfucker, addiction, that had also stolen both my parents, directly and indirectly. I wish my emotional tank was less empty that day, and that I had been able to be more empathetic toward her. Kinder. But like her, I was out of words, spent, with little left to give. It never occurred to me that day that addiction was her full-time job, and her burden was nearly too heavy to carry.

The Shrilling

After a busy day of work and middle school, my son Samson and I drove to the hair salon for much overdue haircuts. Samson was only twelve, but already had a strong sense of personal style. He insisted on growing out his dark blonde hair, so when running down the basketball court, his thick waterfall of hair flowed behind him. That cape of hair may have protected him, given him special powers, and kept him far away from any girls named Delilah. Though at 12, staying away from any girl was something he was becoming less interested in. We had entered the Axe Body Spray years.

We each got our hair washed, conditioned, cut, and styled and debated which overpriced hair products to buy. It was late for a school night, after 8:00pm, and we were impatient to get home to homework and laundry. We left the salon and got into my blue Saab, commenting that the seats were chilly. This was before I could afford a car with seat warmers. It was October, and outside the city, after sunrise and before sunset, we could sometimes hear the boom and echo of hunters' rifles; I imagined the sound of ducks and geese falling out of the sky. The cooling air carried the scent of rotted leaves, bonfire smoke, and natural death. We held our breath and waited for the onset of winter. It would punish us for the next six months.

Though it was getting late in the evening and I was tired,

I loved spending time with Samson, even running mundane errands like this. He was such a great kid and I was so proud of him. I slowly drove through the nearly deserted strip mall parking lot, watching papery leaves anxiously skitter past the vet's office, Walgreens, and the grocery store. At the exit, I mimicked a stop and turned left onto Duluth Street. Over the next block, I gradually accelerated to the full speed limit of 40 mph, with thoughts of work projects and parent-teacher conferences filling my head.

Then I saw it. A flicker of tan to my left, at the soft edge of my peripheral vision. A deer, a good-sized buck, charged onto the street in front of my car. I couldn't react fast enough. My foot couldn't remember how to stop. There was a sickening thud of muscular body meeting metal, the front of the 3,000-pound Saab plowing into the deer's chest and hindquarters, a math and physics problem no one wants to solve. But my mind registered that the deer didn't look right. It looked too big, too long. As my brain processed, I realized there was not one deer. There were two. A second deer, a doe, had been racing slightly behind the buck and met the same fate. The left headlight spotlighted her right before it hit her and sent her tumbling into the street. A third deer glanced off the now-slowed car, lightly stepped around the felled deer in the street, and wobbled and loped into the woods. A noise shaped like a scream garbled out of my throat.

The car had come to a standstill. A mid-toned alarm was dinging, deep inside the dash. I checked to make sure Samson was unhurt, then quickly evaluated myself. No broken bones, no bleeding. The windshield was cracked. Puffs of steam fogged the front of the car. I unclicked my seatbelt and gently pushed open the car door. I told Samson, stay in the car. I wasn't sure what I was going to see when I got out. I heard them before I saw them. Heartbreaking noises of agony came from the front and side of the car. My hands shook. I pulled my chunky Nokia phone from my pocket and fumbled to press the buttons to summon the police.

The deer were sprawled on the cold asphalt, tan and white with splotches of red highlighted by the ghost of the headlights. Their brown eyes were wild and seeking. Neither deer had died from its injuries. Their limbs pointed in unnatural directions. They were shrilling. That's what deer screaming is called. Shrilling.

We weren't far from the police station, and an officer and a community service officer arrived in a few minutes. There were lights but no sirens. Animal injuries aren't rewarded with the sound of urgency. The officer parked his car in front of mine to block motorists from running over the deer. The young community service officer parked behind me, lights flashing, to keep motorists from running into the Saab. He shrugged into a lime-colored florescent vest that was several sizes too large and grabbed his heavy flashlight to redirect what little traffic there was.

The deer were stuck in the uncharted space between life and death. They could not go backward, could not move swiftly into a welcome release. I could sense the deer beseeching. They were begging to die. Their front legs were twisted like tawny ropes. The tips of the buck's sand-colored antlers slowly scraped the asphalt with every move of his head. And the shrilling. It was heartbreaking and it made me want to vomit.

The officer asked me how fast I was driving, and where I was going, and recorded my answers on his silver clipboard. He asked if I had meant to hit the deer. My god, who intends to hit a deer? I answered each question, with tears tracking my cheeks. I started to feel a little unhinged by the sounds of the animals struggling to die, five feet away.

Then I asked, no, I begged the officer to shoot the deer and end the animals' misery. I asked more than once. Every time, he responded that he could not discharge his firearm within the city, to dispatch an animal, no matter how badly injured. I was soaked with flop sweat, adrenaline, and dreadful empathy for the deer.

Samson seemed to be somewhat less affected by the scene. He understood it was an accident, and that nothing could have been done to avoid it. There was no blame to be hung around anyone's neck. While hunting with my husband Steven, Samson had seen a dead deer strung up in a tree in deer camp, waiting for the blood to drain from the carcass. Even at his young age, he better understood the death of deer. The nature of things. But each time I looked at the animals I started to cry again. My hysteria was beginning to unnerve him, and Samson had his window down and repeatedly told me not to look. I didn't listen.

The officer finally said he had everything he needed for his report, and if the car was in good enough shape, I could drive it the few miles home. He handed me a yellow copy of the white report he had taken. He said he was not going to issue me a citation. For what? Accidently murdering a deer or two deer? For asking him to put a bullet in their brains? He told me he called the DNR and they would come and take care of the situation. I was free to go.

I got back in the car. The community service officer pulled around me, no red and blue lights streaking into the night from the roof lightbar, no need to quickly get back to the station, or wherever he was going next.

I tentatively backed up the Saab. I could see the scene: the full, broken bodies of the deer on the asphalt, chests heaving, tortured breath puffing into the cold night, death rattle, dimly lit now only by a streetlight. I put the car in drive and pulled into the right lane. During the slow, slow drive home, Samson comforted me. A child should never have to comfort the parent. That made me feel so much worse. Guiltier. Ashamed. My job was to be the protector, not the victim. I never wanted him to feel unsafe or not heard. He was twelve years old. I was equal parts in shock from the accident and angry at my behavior. I felt selfish.

I pulled into our driveway and clicked open the garage door. My husband, Steven, was waiting for us on the back steps, with every light in the garage on. I vaguely remember calling him, or maybe Samson did. When I squeak-opened my car door, Steven tried to make a little joke about how I was a much better deer hunter than he was. I didn't laugh. As I came around to the front of the Saab, there were bits of coarse tan hair clinging to the grille, wedged in where the left turn signal light used to be. Thin lines of blood and deep metallic creases and dents created a misshapen approximation of the front end. The latch had sprung. The hood had separated from the car itself as if waiting for a strong wind to take flight. The car would never be the same. Neither would I. For years, I would hear the shrilling. I could never make it stop.

CARDINAL POSITION

North, south, east, west; used for giving directions and information from the ground or air in describing the path of travel.

Migration: El Paso 1999

For as long as I could remember, it seemed there was always someone in my family planning a road trip. Charting a penciled path in the road atlas, filling the ancient green Coleman coolers with ice packs, sandwiches, and drinks, cracking open a bag of Fritos, and announcing it was time to go.

What felt like freedom to the adults, the drivers, felt confining and restrictive from the right side of the backseat. It was only later in my adulthood that I understood the promise of "somewhere else."

In the early summer of 1999, two years before our mother died, five years before my divorce, my brother Tim and I both needed a change of scenery. We decided to take a road trip. For Tim, the obvious choice was El Paso, Texas. He wanted to visit Chris, always known to me as Vandy, the kid (to me, he'll always be a kid) who lived next door to us growing up. Tim and Vandy had been fast friends since before preschool, with the added convenience of being only a driveway apart. They participated in all the usual childhood boy shenanigans—firecrackers, sneaking around in the woods, that kind of stuff. Life at home for both of them was challenging, in the same, and different, ways. There was alcohol in common, money worries, and parents who could not resolve anything in a normal tone of voice. There was often uncomfortable silence at our house, and from Vandy's house, we could frequently hear the yelling, especially during the summer, with the windows open. Tim and Vandy were partners in friendship, and one time, partners in crime.

The most memorable mischief they got into was when they were in seventh grade, and they did what boys do after they completed their Minnesota gun safety course. They got BB guns. They loved those brown and black rifle-style guns and were so excited to have them, hold them, and use them. Both sets of parents sternly warned them not to shoot any living things, or put holes in their bedroom walls. As with all young people with developing brains, the advice ran through their heads and flew out the other side.

One summer day, the inevitable happened. One of them shot the other. It was a normal summer day, with not much to do, before we had cable, before the internet. The boys were too young to drive and too old for the playground. Vandy's parents were busy, likely teaching summer school or giving piano lessons in the living room. The boys were going to hang out until they could think of something else to do.

Tim had walked next door and was standing in the doorway to Vandy's room, when Vandy yelled, "FREEZE," with his new BB gun pointed at the doorway. Before Tim knew what was going on, Vandy proceeded to shoot at him with his BB gun. Multiple times. If it had been a real gun with bullets, Tim would have died. As it was, he was in a good amount of pain, after the shock wore off. Tim walked back home and told my mother what happened. The next stop was the pediatrician, with painful BB extractions, and getting an earful about gun safety from Dr. Schulenberg.

After Tim got home from the doctor, his wounds bandaged, and bored once again, he and Vandy went skateboarding around the neighborhood. Then a police car rolled up near them and stopped. The officer asked, "Which dumbass shot the other one?" He suggested they might want to take the gun safety course again. Before he left, he told them sternly not to do it (shoot each other) again. And that was the end of the law enforcement intervention.

Vandy was on the receiving end of an epic tongue-lashing by his father that night, and maybe more. Through the open windows we could hear his father, Jay, bellowing. Tim, being the victim and not the shooter, got less, but words were spoken by my father with intensity and gravitas. As kids, Tim and I were both more scared of what our tall father with the deep voice might do, than what he actually did. I'm sure Vandy would also want me to mention that Tim was the one who loaded Vandy's gun with BBs earlier, not that it impacted the outcome.

Though they took different paths after high school, Tim and Vandy stayed good friends. Vandy left to attend college in northern Minnesota and my brother stayed in town and worked for my parents in their small business. Like his parents, Vandy got a degree in education and wanted to teach. He moved to El Paso for a job, as the weather there was good and the cost of living was attractive. By the time we visited, several years later, Vandy was married; he and his wife had a baby and a cute house in the El Paso suburbs. He had built a new life for himself in the desert, far away from our small town and the influence of his parents.

Tim consulted with Vandy, and I negotiated with my then-husband Chris to parent our son Samson, solo for a long weekend. Our father generously offered to finance a portion of the trip. With his COPD worsening his long road trip days were sadly behind him.

Tim and I started our El Paso journey on an early-morning flight from Minneapolis to Albuquerque. The plan was to drive to El Paso from Albuquerque, because Tim loved to drive, and it was cheaper. But mostly we drove simply because Tim loved to drive. I had gone to college in New Mexico and knew well the desolate stretch of I-25 we would be traveling. I was not a fan.

After landing in Albuquerque, we secured our black Infiniti G20 rental sedan, a fancy upgrade, thanks to our father. We hopped in and embarked on the four-hour trip south. In that car, we talked about things that were not open for discussion ever while we were in Minnesota. In that car, we could look out the window while we talked. There was no eye contact. There were no facial expressions to decode. It was akin to a confessional at seventy mph.

We talked about our father's health, his worsening COPD; his ongoing drinking, which we could not absolutely confirm because he was sneakier about it since he went to treatment in the late 1980s; and our mother's drinking, which was obvious to everyone and getting worse by the year. All you had to do was look at her, and the deep wrinkles, hand tremors, and bloodshot eyes telegraphed how deeply unwell she was. We lived with a belly-deep fear that she would get in the car, drive into something or off something and die, or injure or kill someone else. We were pre-living with the guilt of that. Tim tried to drive her everywhere, and it was exhausting. What we didn't say was that we were both terrified of her drinking herself to death. It felt inevitable and sad. Even in the desert heat, the car felt clammy with hopelessness.

We talked about my marriage, which was starting to show early signs of fraying. We talked about Tim staying in the same small town where he grew up, feeling yoked and guilted by my parents' ongoing financial support. They needed care, and Tim was the one they counted on to do it. To do everything. He could not leave. They made sure of that, but Tim couldn't see it that way. He was in a cage lined with our parents' money. He couldn't see or wouldn't acknowledge that, either. We talked about our grandmother, Eleanor, who died earlier in the year, just shy of her 89th birthday. Barely five feet tall, she was a force, and she left a deep hole in our lives. She danced a jig at her 80th birthday party, the same party she invited people to by placing an ad in the local newspaper. She was the family's connective tissue, our true matriarch. She was bossy and tough and commanded all of us from her built-up orthopedic shoes, and pointed the way with her cane.

We were related to half of Goodhue County, the clan-like O'Neill, Farrell, Tri, and Doyle families on her side, and the Gielow and Mandelkow families on my grandfather's side. My grandmother saw it as her duty to try to keep everyone in line. We were sad at her passing, but we laughed about some of her antics as we drove along.

New Mexico was summer-brown and dusty, there was not much to see on that long drive south, and even worse radio reception. Tim half-heartedly complained that we didn't stop to see White Sands, but I was anxious to get to El Paso and had no interest in being stuck on the side of the road at night if something went wrong. We finally got to El Paso late in the day and found Vandy's house pretty easily with our MapQuest printout.

Tim and I planned to spend Thursday and Friday driving around and then seeing my college friend, Karen, who lived in nearby Las Cruces. It was fun reconnecting with her over a delicious lunch and beer. Every place we ate in El Paso had wonderful food. I had left New Mexico nine years earlier, and I appreciated the flavors and spices that were lacking in Minnesota, as well as the sopapillas with honey that I had never found in the Midwest.

When we got up on Saturday morning, Vandy suggested we go to Juarez, Mexico, just over the border. He said there were fun things to do there, and the beer was very cheap. Having never been there, the adventure sounded great to us. Vandy never mentioned it, and we were completely unaware that Juarez was far less safe than he let on. In fact, 200+ women had been murdered in Juarez over the six previous years. This was due largely to the growing power of the Juarez Cartel and the simmering drug wars. Maybe if I had known that, I would not have gone to Juarez, or I might have been less independent and stuck closer to Tim and Vandy. But we never talked about it, and I did my thing.

    That warm Saturday morning, we hopped into Vandy's little blue car, or rather, my brother slowly folded his 6'7" frame into the front seat, and Vandy and I hopped in and buckled our seatbelts. We had a couple of bottles of water with us, and we headed for the border. Tim had offered to drive the Infiniti, but Vandy said that was just asking for trouble. As we pulled out of his neighborhood and got on the highway, we asked if we, or he, since he was driving, needed anything special to drive into Mexico. Vandy laughed and told us there was no way he was driving his car into Juarez. It was a terrible idea, he said, due to rampant theft, awful roads, and difficulty getting back across the border with a vehicle. He said the line could be hours long because they now checked every car for drugs. He had even seen the US Border Patrol take apart a car, leaving the frame, the hood, and a stack of doors sitting on the ground, as the driver and passengers were handcuffed and led away.

    By late morning, we arrived at the US side of the border. We could see the border patrol station, with its Texas and US flags flown high, and numerous border agents walking around in front of the building. It was also not hard to spot the enforcement agents, with their military-type uniforms and machine-type guns. Vandy found a place to park in a paid lot nearby, under the bridge that spanned the Rio Grande.

Vandy locked the car, and we set off walking toward Mexico. There was no waiting line to cross to the Mexico side, and with little fanfare, we followed the markings on the sidewalk, paid a few pesos, and crossed the Paso del Norte bridge into Mexico. "Welcome to Juarez!" Vandy said.

The difference between El Paso and Juarez was stark. We had crossed into a different country and a very different way of life. It was jarring. High-pitched motorcycles weaved down the busy, narrow streets, sometimes with two or more people on the back, each clutching the waist of the person in front of them. Drivers of white panel trucks honked and screamed out their windows in rapid Spanish. On the road, there were areas missing asphalt, with deep potholes filled with dirty water. Skinny brown dogs with brown eyes and long whip tails roamed everywhere. Walking down the main street in the late-summer heat, we would regularly catch a whiff of meat cooking, garbage, body odor. It reminded me a little bit of Jamaica, once you strayed from the resorts, and went into the hills and the small towns. There was no slick veneer, no high walls with smiling people, no sanitized version, no piped-in music for the tourists. There was no illusion of joy. There was only commerce and life and poverty.

As we walked, we stuck close to Vandy, since it was clear he knew where he was going, and he was the veteran border-crosser among us. He also knew a good bit of Spanish, far more than we did. All I remembered was kitchen Spanish, picked up when I waitressed in college. Knowing chinga tu madre, or puta, or ojete, would not be especially useful.

Most of the people around us were speaking Spanish. But many of the signs on the bars, stores, tattoo shops, pharmacies, and restaurants were either in Spanish and English or only English. It was clear this area was well-primed for US tourists and the dollars they brought over the border. Like other border towns, we also saw many off-duty US military personnel, obvious with their short haircuts and stiff posture, drinking beer at the outdoor bars.

Vandy finally led us to our destination, a large white-canopied outdoor seating area, on an expanse of asphalt, that looked to be a huge bar. As we walked up, we heard the fast accordion music of the Música Nortena blaring from speakers, clanking of empty beer bottles, and men yelling in English. There was faded red lettering on the wall outside the place, something about beer and tacos and dancing. We were ushered to a plastic table by a smiling host in a polo shirt, made ourselves comfortable in our chairs, and ordered the first round of Coronas. There was even a 2-for-1 special, so we were off to the races at 10:30 am. A red basket of salty, greasy, warm chips and a dish of salsa was dropped off with the beer. It was pleasant under that canopy, protected from the already pounding sun. Tim was a little concerned about not speaking Spanish. Vandy said, "All you need to know is *uno mas cerveza por favor*, and *baño*! Or just say beer and toilet, they'll know what you mean."

With each subsequent delivery of beers, the friendly waiter replenished our basket of chips and black bowl of red salsa. After a couple of rounds, I ordered a bottle of Coke. I was bored, and already tired of the music, the beer, the men yelling. Vandy said there was a nice store just around the corner, and a craft market somewhere around, and suggested I should go check them out.

I left the guys sitting under the canopy, with more beers on the way, and wandered around a few of the Juarez backstreets, until I found the store Vandy was talking about. I spent an hour in the store, looking at the silver jewelry, pottery, woven rugs, and lace tablecloths on offer. I found some nice placemats, and negotiated a price for them, using the international language of "calculator" that my mother had taught me. I headed back to the white canopy, purchase in hand. I got lost once, and I never found the craft market. I eventually found the guys, and it was clear that the beer delivery had continued. We had been in Juarez for hours and they were having a much better time than I was. It was deep into the afternoon, so I suggested maybe we could eat something besides chips, and then get going. Tim and Vandy made it clear I was the buzzkill, just as it was also clear that I would be doing the driving, once we got back over the border. We wolfed down some tacos, paid the tab, and headed back toward the border. It took us a while to navigate there since I didn't know exactly where it was, and the guys were busy trying not to stumble into potholes or step in clumps of dog shit.

We finally got to the border station. The line was much longer and much slower to get out of Mexico than it was to get in. It looked like the US border agents were stopping each person, asking them questions and checking IDs. It took me a while to notice, but anyone with any shade of brown skin was detained quite a bit longer, only addressed in English, no joking, and had their documents thoroughly scrutinized. Tim, Vandy, and I stood in line, the late-day sun beating on us, and stayed within the painted markings on the sidewalk. An agent with a visible gun paced back and forth, closely watching the people waiting in line, and admonished anyone who stepped outside the markings.

When we got close to the front of the line, we started digging for our driver's licenses. That's all we needed to get back into the United States. In a hushed and pressured tone, Vandy said, "Shit you guys, I don't have my ID!" He had left it on the kitchen table, in the flurry of leaving the house. We tried to think of solutions, like calling Vandy's wife to bring the ID, since I had my flip phone. The problem was, we knew she wasn't home. And I was pretty sure my phone wouldn't work in Mexico. Tim and I thought of going across the border, driving to the house, finding the ID, driving back to the border, crossing into Mexico, and handing Vandy the ID. But that could take hours. It was clear that Vandy was anxious about potentially having to stay the night in Juarez. The border station was not open 24 hours, so he would have to find a by-the-hour hotel or other place to ride out the night.

Everyone was much more sober at this point, and we came up with our plan. The three of us would go across the border, standing together, tightly, with Vandy in the middle. If stopped, we would just "vouch" for Vandy, assuring the border officer that he was indeed an American citizen. That plan sounds ridiculous now, but it was 1999. All three of us were blonde, in Vandy's case, white-blonde, blue-eyed, with very white skin, and flat Midwestern accents. We didn't understand the huge amount of capital and privilege that was afforded us, especially in that part of the country, at that time. It was pre-9/11, so there was far less scrutiny or level of security than we have now. We just assumed it would be fine. No big deal.

As we got closer to the front of the line, we tried not to look nervous. At that point, the agents were letting some people through, checking the IDs of others, and leading some unlucky folks away for a more thorough screening. They seemed to be chosen randomly. When it was our turn, Tim and I each took a deep breath, proffered our IDs at the same time, and said, "Oh, he's with us," (meaning Vandy). The officer looked at the three of us, wobblily wedged together, sweating from more than just the heat. He looked each of us in the eye, and then finally waved us through. In a few more steps, we were back on American soil. We stared straight ahead until we walked out of the border entry area, and onto the hot tarmac in front of the building. We took some shaky breaths, panting a little from the tension, and shook our heads at the success of our audacious caper. We were still too scared to laugh. The border crossing process, with its long, snaking line, had taken us quite a long time, and in the early twilight, it took us a while to find Vandy's little blue car under the overpass. He handed me the keys to drive. I got us lost, maybe twice, but it didn't even matter.

    The next day, Tim and I put our bags into the black Infiniti and headed back to Albuquerque for our flight home. Part way into the drive, we thought we had a flat tire, but it turned out to just be the wind, yanking us both east and west. Tim didn't complain about not stopping at White Sands, and I didn't complain about the crappy place where we ate lunch. The AC sliced through the dry heat, but the sun was still relentless, pouring itself onto our arms as we drove.

    Whatever had facilitated our deep and candid conversation on the way down to El Paso had evaporated on the return trip. We stuck to superficial topics like the heat and how good the food was. Neither of us launched into anything of consequence. It felt like some sort of magical portal was now closed. It felt like the trip was bifurcated into a before and an after. On the way down to El Paso, we somehow felt free to talk, to share, to speculate. That was the first time I remember that ever happening. Tim and I were more than six years apart in age, almost a whole generation. We loved each other, of course, and would protect one another. But until that first day in the car, I don't think we had the closeness or trust in one another to have that type of authentic conversation. I had only recently told him about the childhood abuse. I blurted it out as we were walking across a grocery store parking lot. We hadn't spoken of it again.

Growing up, there was always talking, lots of talking, around the dinner table and on the phone. My mother, especially, was a talker. But much of the dinnertime conversation was about my parents' business. Much of it was about other people. What I found so strange growing up, though, is how much the few friends I had loved my parents. Trusted them. How many times they sat on the end of my parents' king-sized bed and cried, deep in the evening, told my parents their troubles, and sought advice, especially in high school. I mean, my parents overall were nice and caring and generous people. I felt a little smug that my friends liked my parents more than their own. But I also felt a streak of white-hot jealousy when my parents were doting on my friends, and I was on the sidelines, stoking the fires of my deep secrets, of my lies. I felt very confused.

After the openness we had driving to El Paso, I felt optimistic we could continue our dialog. That there was a definite thawing in the hot desert. On the drive back, I realized that I was incredibly hungry for connection. I wanted more. I had so many things I wanted to tell Tim. My terror had decreased to just feeling scared about how he would react when he knew more about me. When he saw the depth of my weirdness. My brokenness. But that didn't happen, even when I tried to ask some leading questions. I tried talking about the peculiar experience of sailing through Border Patrol. I tried talking about how our grandpa drove a school bus route through the nearby Indian reservation in the 1970s, and how Juarez reminded me a little of Prairie Island at that time. A tough place with people just trying to survive.

Looking back, I think I was trying to extract data from our conversations to winnow and shape and better understand my own identity—understand our family and my place in it. I had not yet started therapy and had not yet pried the lid off my trauma. I didn't understand how the world worked differently for untraumatized people. I was not self-aware enough to understand that my whiteness was the shield that protected me, especially at the border. If you had asked me at that time what it was like to be privileged, I would have laughed. That was the last way I would have described myself.

In the car, Tim and I talked about how it was clear that Vandy had made El Paso his home, and he was never moving back to Minnesota. Tim might have felt a little disappointed, but again, he did not share those thoughts with me.

We got closer to Albuquerque and talked of heading home. I'm not convinced either of us was sure what home was, beyond words and a concept. But we did our best and flew back to what at least was familiar. To the place where people counted on us and needed us. To our obligations. Parents, child, spouse. One day, maybe, we would figure out what home was or meant to us. Neither of us was ready. Whatever version of home felt the most true to me, I had learned, always meant having to say goodbye. I was very skilled at doing just that.

The Brown Jug

I could never quite figure out if my parents were racist. At least outwardly, they seemed to be pretty accepting of people, no matter their race, or color. But, there were times when the mask slipped a bit, and conversations would light up about "those people," and how "they" lived. A bit of scorn about what people without money or resources or agency did to make ends meet, like using government programs. That was ironic, as my parents both grew up very poor, and I'm sure difficult and courageous choices were made in their families to keep everyone fed. It has been curious to me, too, how people so well-traveled could still have an arms-length relationship with the "other."

My parents loved to travel. They were not especially picky about where they, and by extension, we went. When I was a kid, the only constraints were how much time and money we had, as usually both were in short supply. My father loved road trips, truck stops, and lemon pie, and would pull out the Rand McNally road atlas and chart our journey in pencil. We road-tripped everywhere from Alabama to Alaska, with the green metal Coleman cooler in the back, a bag filled with Hershey bars and Fritos, and the tan Thermos of coffee for my father up front. In later years, my parent started to favor flying, cruises, and all-inclusive resorts. They loved the fact that they could hop on a plane in the harsh Minnesota winter, and a few hours later, be deposited in balmy, sanitized versions of Mexico or the Caribbean.

My parents were genuinely curious people. They wanted to understand and appreciate how and where folks lived in the towns and villages beyond the high walls of the resorts and hotels. My mother, Margaret, was the more social of the two, so it was not unusual for her to chat up the staff on day one, and ask their names and life stories, within a few days of arriving. I'm sure it was tiring for the staff. When she came home and showed us photos, she always referred to the waiters or waitresses or butlers as her new friends.

My mother had trouble with boundaries and would ask the staff question after question, each time drinks were delivered, and there were many. As my parents stretched out on their loungers by the pool, in Mazatlán, or on the cruise ship, before my father handed over the dollar tip for each round of drinks, my mother would ask the server about where they lived, how they lived, what they ate, how many kids they had, what they did for fun. She spoke no Spanish, aside from *gracias* and *por favor*, and would exclaim how friendly everyone was in Mazatlán, as the servers smiled and nodded at her in the hot sun.

At one point, my parents were planning to build a winter house in Zihuatanejo, Mexico. That plan got derailed by my father's COPD diagnosis, coupled with his secret drinking, and my mother's progressive alcoholism. That didn't stop their winter vacations, and they made Jamaica the new favorite. They were completely enamored with the balmy winter weather, the beaches, and the warmth and kindness of the people. My parents visited many times, raved about their experiences, and made my brother and me look at endless, repetitive photos of palm trees, beaches, rum drinks, and arts and crafts, every time they came home.

My father also loved Jamaican food. He regaled us with descriptions of the jerk meat that was on every menu, as long as you were outside the resorts. "I can have spaghetti at home, but the jerk chicken and pork and fish are special. Spicy, but not too hot for me. Jamaican rice and peas sure stick to your ribs." In the photos of food, taken in dark restaurants, with poor lighting and a cheap camera, the food looked less appetizing than what he described. There were brown lumps of indeterminate grilled meat, accompanied by scoops of clumpy white rice, dotted with what must have been peas. And always bottles of Red Stripe, or sweating glasses of rum punch.

When my son Samson was three, my parents treated us—Samson, my then-husband, and me— to a week-long trip to Jamaica. My father, despite his shortcomings, was a truly generous man. Case in point: Whenever he ate in a restaurant with anyone— friends, neighbors, relatives— he was quick, really quick, to pick up the check. He and I got into some pretty serious "slap Jack" moments when I reached for the black vinyl book with the restaurant check, especially at Weiderholdt's Supper Club, outside my small hometown. He was a proud man, and in some strange way, his love language, like mine, was feeding people.

When he and my mother invited us to Jamaica, it would have been ridiculous to refuse. We didn't have much money at that time, and visiting a tropical island during the Minnesota winter was so far beyond our reach that we almost couldn't believe we were going, and were excited, even with the challenges that traveling with a toddler could bring. I packed and repacked our suitcases, but didn't think to consult or buy a guidebook. I had been looking at my parents' photos for more than a decade and thought I knew the place. I had seen the lovely beaches, frilly hibiscus flowers, and smiling people awaiting us.

The only travel issue we had to work around was my father's health because his emphysema was getting worse. His lungs could no longer inflate and deflate the way he needed them to. He required oxygen for the long flight from Minnesota, and in Jamaica, he needed to cart around little tanks. We also brought his wheelchair, for the times he didn't feel like walking. Those times were becoming more and more frequent. My parents were booked in TWA first class for the flights to Jamaica and back. The first leg to St. Louis went smoothly. On the connecting flight to Montego Bay, the airline did not load the special in-flight oxygen we had requested weeks earlier. There was much discussion, raised voices, and showing of receipts, and the captain was summoned. My father perched in his vinyl airplane seat, sweating and starting to panic, as his body craved the sweetness of oxygen. A compromise was reached, albeit an embarrassing one for my father. Every plane carries several canisters of emergency oxygen, for in-flight emergencies. My father would use one of those canisters, with the large plastic face mask, rather than the less conspicuous, small nose cannulas he was used to. The flight took off, and we arrived in Jamaica without incident.

    My father had arranged for us to have a car and driver in Jamaica. As we walked out of the airport and into the wall of humidity, we spied a man holding a white piece of paper with MIKE G written on it in black marker. As we walked up, the driver, in a tan shirt and dark brown pants, smiled and introduced himself as Nelson. He led us to his light brown van, which was old but clean, and we loaded up and set off for Ocho Rios. Nelson had already picked up the first of my father's many tanks of oxygen. The sun was setting by the time we got to the hotel, after a bumpy nearly two-hour drive from the Montego Bay airport. We arrived at our big pink hotel and got settled in our rooms, one for my parents, and one for the three of us.

    At dinner, my father announced that we would be going to town several times during the trip. My father was not an excitable man, but that night, he was as eager and enthusiastic as he got. He was in his element - he was in Jamaica and he was on vacation. He wanted us to see Jamaica the way he saw it, through the people, the food, and the music. He was thrilled young Samson was along. As a new mother, I was worried about the water, the food, the bugs, the sun, and strangers. How would we keep our tow-headed three-year-old protected? I didn't voice those concerns, or not very loudly, as my father was quite enthused, and I didn't want to bring down the mood.

The next morning at the hotel, my father informed us that we were having lunch in town. We were going to the Ocho Rios Jerk Centre, which I assumed was a local café. I asked if there were things Samson could eat, and he assured me there were.

Nelson was waiting for us at the entrance of the hotel, and he asked my father if he was sure he wanted to go there, to the Jerk Centre, and got a confident, "Yep!" After a short drive, we pulled up to the restaurant— well, not a restaurant, more like red and white plastic tables and chairs arranged in a parking lot, partially under a large dirty white canopy. There were half a dozen cats and several scrawny brown dogs roaming the space, pausing hopefully at the occupied tables. Samson wanted to pet all of them, but his grandfather sternly told him no, and that was that. My father rarely said no to Samson about anything, so when he did, it made an impression, and there was no arguing. The seating area was marinating in thick gray smoke blowing off huge outdoor grills. We watched waves of that pimento wood smoke as it billowed with the trade winds.

We found a table out of the direct path of the smoke, and my mother invited Nelson to join us for lunch. He tried to decline, but my mother was very insistent, as usual. My father was a study in happiness, sitting in a plastic chair, under that canopy, which was surprising, as we didn't often see him that way. Even with the smoke making his lungs clatter and work, he had the look of a man who was exactly where he wanted to be. He read out all the choices from the chalkboard menu above a plywood counter with a cash register sitting on it. My father suggested the jerk chicken for us, with some rice and peas, and ordered chicken and pork for himself, my mother, and Nelson. Nelson suggested extra rice and peas for Samson, just in case he found the chicken a bit spicy. We ordered green bottles of Ting grapefruit soda for the three of us, and squat bottles of Red Stripe beer for my parents and Nelson.

When our order was called, Nelson retrieved the food, heaped on paper plates and in Styrofoam boxes. I told Samson to wait before he took some chicken – I wanted to judge the spice level. The meat smelled delicious, if a little peppery. I picked up a drumstick and took a big bite. Seconds later, I felt, and no doubt looked, like a cartoon character, with my eyes flying out from my face, ah-ooh-ga! My face turned blotchy pink, then red, then glowed like a stop sign. My eyes watered, and small tears may have rolled down my face. A mantle of sweat crawled across my face, starting from my upper lip. I chewed slowly, and I couldn't decide whether I should swallow the chicken or spit it out.

Good Midwestern manners won out, and I swallowed the chicken. I felt my throat tighten a little, and my esophagus felt like I swallowed a road flare. I grabbed for the Ting, and Nelson said,

"No! Eat the rice! Eat the rice!" I shoveled forkful after forkful into my mouth until the pain receded, and I could once again see clearly.

During this whole demonstration, my father laughed. Not snickered, not chuckled, but laughed, loudly, finally trailing off into, "Woo hoo, now that was funny," followed by a few minutes of coughing. He was thoroughly entertained. Nelson asked if it was my first trip to Jamaica, and after I nodded, he proceeded to give me a few helpful tips – take the skin off the chicken, eat smaller bites, don't drink the Ting, that makes it worse, advice I really could have used about five minutes earlier. My father was still chuckling when he tucked into his meal, ignoring the devil's side eye I was giving him. He was very tall but very skinny. The COPD had diminished his appetite over the years, so I had to admit, it was nice to see him eating so eagerly.

After lunch, we relaxed in the van with full bellies, and a salty breeze rolled over us from open windows. Nelson took us for an extended scenic drive along the ocean. The roads were a mix of paved and pocked, and Nelson did a great job maneuvering around the largest holes. We saw smoke rising from the fields and smelled burning grass and garbage. Near one of the small villages along the road, someone was burning tires, and we rolled up the windows to seal out the thick black smoke.

As we bumped along, Nelson pointed out the Golden Eye 007 house, where Ian Fleming lived while writing his James Bond novels. He also happily gave his opinions on which hotels were

"Jamaican nice" but not "American nice," and pointed out the places with the worst tippers. Germans! He dropped us off at our hotel, saying he would see us the next day.

The next morning was lightly hazy, with the promise of sun later in the day. My parents planned to sleep in and order breakfast from room service. With a three-year-old, there was no such thing as sleeping in. Samson, Chris, and I ate in the restaurant, and after breakfast, we walked toward the beach. Samson was excited about the ocean and swimming, so we said we'd take a look. As we got closer to the water, we discovered a photo shoot for a Canadian shoe company getting set up, complete with lights, a director, several child actors, and even a supermodel, who was waiting under a red umbrella, looking bored. As we were looking around, a production assistant walked up to us, and said young Samson, with his thick blond hair and big smile, would be a great addition to their photo shoot. He asked if we would give permission, and told us we could sit nearby and watch. We signed some forms, and watched as our three-year-old had his hair professionally styled, and smiled on command. He was paid twenty-five dollars, in cash. We lazed at the beach and pool for the rest of the day.

My parents mentioned we were going out to dinner at a local place that night, and to wear something casual. Nelson was waiting for us, again in his tan dress shirt and dark brown pants. His shirt was the same color as the van, he appeared to melt into the door as he leaned against it. When asked for our dinner destination, my father told him, "Somewhere authentic. Like real Jamaican food. Last time we were here, we went to The Brown Jug." Nelson shook his head and asked my father if he was sure. My father said, "Yep, I'm sure. Let's go." Nelson frowned and told my father that The Brown Jug was really for locals, not tourists. My father dug in his heels. Nelson shrugged, as if to say, you're the boss.

The sun was setting and we were hungry as we piled in the van. Once outside the hotel property, we noticed that there were fewer streetlights, and as we left the outskirts of Ocho Rios, there were none at all. The van's yellowed headlights were ineffective in pushing away the darkness, but remarkably, Nelson seemed to sense when a dog, person, or motorcycle was going to appear from the side of the road, and he double-tapped the horn sending out two quick blasts. There were no mishaps. We drove along the coast, windows down again, breathing in damp salty air combined with a good amount of fine road dust. After what felt like a long time, but was probably only 20 minutes, Nelson slowed down, and turned into a sandy dirt parking lot, casually delineated by rows of strategically placed rocks and cemented coral. "We're here!" he announced.

In the backseat, we exchanged looks. I looked out the window and fought the urge to quickly roll it up. "Here" was a small, shabby whitewashed building, in the middle of nowhere, plopped on a spot in the sand. There were no lights in the parking area, except for some faded Christmas lights strung between two poles, A single light bulb illuminated the hand-painted sign on the side of the building. It read The Brown Jug in brown letters with a small drawing of a jug at a jaunty angle. There were two old sedans huddled together in the vicinity of the front door. I felt a tickle of apprehension. Glancing at my mother, I could tell she was feeling the same way. We both looked at my father, and his face was set, impassive, neutral. I thought to myself, great, we're all going to get murdered because my father wanted some "authentic" fish.

We got out of the van, Samson holding my hand tightly. I could hear my mother murmuring to my father in a quiet but urgent way. He ignored her and slowly walked forward, deliberately, leaving our little group behind and clumped together for safety. The entrance door was dimly lit with more colorful Christmas lights, and we stepped inside, Nelson leading the way. As we were walking in, we heard a low buzz of conversation, punctuated by a woman's laugh, and then silence. It was like a movie, where the only sound we heard was water dripping in the sink, and the occasional clink of bottles. Nelson called out to the bartender in quick and loud patois. There was a short exchange, and we got the sense that Nelson was somehow vouching for us.

The inside of The Brown Jug was dark. Not dim, not shadowy, but dark, dark. As my eyes adjusted, I heard some slight shuffling. Lit only by the Christmas lights at the entrance and a few tiny votive candles scattered around the room, I saw flashes of white, moving. They flashed again, in a completely different part of the room. At that point, I realized that the white flashes belonged to eyes and the eyes belonged to people who were sitting at small tables in the room. It was obvious, we were intruders. This was not our place. As our little entourage slowly stumbled along, I could nearly see the outlines of heads, of shoulders, of hands, and I could smell the sweet mix of hair oil and perfume.

It was still deathly silent in the room, and the only noises were coming from our shoes on the sandy floor, and my father's slight gasps and labored breathing. We followed Nelson through the room, and to an open doorway at the back. "Dad! There were people in there, sitting in the dark, and I'm nervous," I stage-whispered. "Those people are here for dinner, nobody's going to bother us," he whispered back. As we walked through the back doorway, I saw several red plastic tables, with matching chairs placed around them in the sand. "Here," said Nelson, as he pushed two tables together. Those tables were also lit by more Christmas lights overhead, attached to a long extension cord. Nelson walked back into the building and came back with a small votive candle for our table, though with the breeze, I wasn't sure it was going to last for long. Nelson said he would wait inside while we ate, and my parents said that was silly, and invited him to join us. It took a very long moment before he agreed. We had no idea the kind of awkward position we were putting him in. We had no concept of the depth of our ignorance, and our lack of cultural awareness. My parents thought they were doing a nice thing, the right thing, by shopping and eating at local places, and inviting Nelson to join us. They, we, never took into account that may have been the last thing he wanted.

    We learned there was no set menu at The Brown Jug, you just inquired as to what they were serving that day. Nelson was the emissary between the inside and the outside, and he relayed what they had on offer– chicken, callaloo, and snapper caught that afternoon. My parents and Nelson ordered snapper and the rest of us ordered chicken, plain please, for Samson. Red Stripes and Ting bottles were delivered, and we chatted awkwardly with Nelson while waiting for the food. Nelson kept glancing at the back entrance, as if he was waiting for someone. My mother's hand trembled as she lifted the Red Stripe to her lips, drained the bottle, and requested another. Samson jabbered about fish and swimming and asked Nelson several times if they had French fries or chicken nuggets.

    To fill space in the strained conversation, I asked Nelson why there were only two cars in front, and maybe a dozen people inside the building. He looked at me like it was the most obvious thing in the world, "It's Jamaica, mon. It's a beautiful country, and we walk, miss." As I processed his words, I felt an uneasy sheen of privilege coat me, like a bad smell. I looked around, at the building, at the tables, at the beach. Nelson ran interference between us and the kitchen, because we didn't belong here, and I was embarrassed. We had intruded, inserted ourselves too far into local culture.

We showed up, waved some money, and went where we wanted. Did what we wanted. I felt a sour mixture of anxiety and shame roll around in my gut. The ocean was in front of us, and while we couldn't see it, the reliable dumping of waves and taking them back was a balm.

Our food arrived on white paper plates, and we started to eat. The chicken was still spicy for our Midwestern palates, even with no skin and tiny bites, so it was slow going. Samson happily enjoyed the rice and peas, though much of it fell off the fork before he could get it to his mouth. There was also a plate of bread, which I learned was called hard do (hard dough). It was a bit sweet and took the peppery edge off the chicken. Halfway through the meal, I looked over at Nelson. He was eating like a man who'd won the lottery. I was stunned by his efficiency in segmenting his snapper, eating the skin, the meat, the insides, and then with great delicacy sucking the remaining morsels off the bones. When he was done, all that remained on his plate was the empty head, a gray ghostly skeleton, and the tail of a fish that hours before had been swimming in the ocean in front of us.

After we finished our meal, Nelson drove us back to the hotel. It was quiet in the van. I was relieved to see the hotel, the buildings, the lights, the people. Safety. Familiarity. I was exhausted and had a lot of thinking to do. I felt something during that meal, at that place, but I could not give it a name. That wouldn't come until many years later. I'm embarrassed to say how long it took. I think it was when George Floyd was murdered. When we all talked a little more openly about whiteness and Blackness and privilege and underrepresented people and inequity. About allyship. For the most part, I had always espoused that I believed in an "I don't see color I see people" philosophy. After George Floyd was murdered, I took a hard look, and I called bullshit on myself. I had to painfully admit my own biases. I have several Black colleagues who I am friendly with. I highly respected them and truly enjoyed their company. They are great people. And I treated them differently. In our non-work conversations, I tried to drop in little tidbits of what I thought of as Black culture, to try to show that I "got it." I brought up Black actors or music. Things in the news. I realized how much of an idiot I was. I still haven't apologized to those colleagues, because I can't get past my mortification.

After Nelson dropped us off at the hotel that night, my father turned and poked me in the shoulder. "Jesus Christ!" he said loudly, "you should have heard yourself telling me there were PEOPLE in the restaurant! And that you were scared of them. The funniest damn thing I've ever heard." He turned to my mother and asked if she had enjoyed the meal. She nodded and glanced over at me. She was marinated in beer, soused, level five drunk – the stage just before the yelling and crying came. But there was a small moment of clarity, and for once I felt she saw me, she understood. I felt like in that tiny moment, she acknowledged my inability and the impossibility of my trying to measure up to my father. I felt she saw us both, more or less clearly. I think she also saw herself, as a player in our ongoing performance. And I felt like she acknowledged the larger, unnamed thing coming from my father, a thin, mean, stubborn current running just below the connection. Then the moment was over, the knowing once again obscured by the alcohol and blind commitment. Samson hugged his grandparents, and we walked to our rooms and retired for the night.

I wish my mother's moment of clarity had lasted longer, had meant more, and had opened up something more lasting between us. I wish she had been sober enough to remember it. I'm sure she had her own set of secrets, and maybe she could find an untapped place of empathy in herself. If that single moment had begun knitting us together then maybe it wouldn't have taken several more years for me to disclose the abuse to her and my father. At that point, I had never told either of my parents about the assaults, the abuse, any of it. I was thirty-one years old. I was ashamed and still held the belief that I was at fault. I was still fragile in that way, and I could not count on either of my parents to be empathetic or understanding. I could not visualize, nor could I trust, that they would take my side, and be angry on my behalf, rather than angry at me.

In some ways, that small moment with my mother in Jamaica, much like the car ride back from El Paso with my brother made things feel worse. I got a glimpse of how things could have been and it felt like it was snatched away. It would have been better if I had never known. If I had not been allowed to hope, just for a minute. I continued to hold my secrets close to my body.

When I Was a Ghost

I was not a person who easily made friends at work. I spent a lot of energy thinking about what to say, and how to act around coworkers. How to fit in. But when I took a job at a big healthcare company, I did make some good friend-like acquaintances. One of my favorites was Shruti.

Shruti was from India, and she and I talked about a lot of things. She was in her late 20s, and marriage was a frequent topic. For more than a year, her parents, who lived 9,000 miles away in India, had been telling her, pushing her, insisting it was time to get married. After being ignored for a year, her parents finally lost patience with her pickiness and apathy toward potential suitors. They hired a matchmaker in Bangalore, who went to work on finding her an acceptable groom. Shruti roundly refused the first match, a man nearly 20 years her senior, but accepted the second, who was closer to her age.

He and Shruti spoke on the phone a few times, had a supervised visit and one public outing, and the wedding date was set for August 2010, in Mangalore. Shruti was excited to plan the wedding and get married, but she rolled her eyes when she talked about the groom. He was rather morose, with black caterpillar eyebrows, and noticeable nose hair. He was in IT, like she was, educated, from a good family, in an acceptable caste. He ticked all the boxes. Her mother told Shruti she would learn to love him. I kept my opinions to myself.

Shruti said he was the opposite of fun. He didn't like to do fun things, like go to parties, or out to dinner. He did not like how independent she was, or the fact that she was a pretty bad cook. He preferred video games to her. He told her this marriage was not his idea. He told her that he did not choose *her*. His parents did.

The wedding plans went into high gear. There were only three months to plan, and there was a lot to do. Shruti flew to India for two weeks to get her wedding outfits and events planned, work with the mothers on the guest list, secure a venue, and a million other details. When she returned to the US, she turned almost everything over to her mother and trusted her to pull off an amazing event, of respectable size and quality per her family's status.

The week before the wedding, I flew into Bangalore and met up with Shruti at the airport. She and I hopped on a Kingfisher Airlines flight to Mangalore, where I was greeted warmly by her family, as an honored guest. It became obvious at our first dinner together, that typical meals in Mangalore were no match for my scared Midwestern palate. Shruti's family had ordered a feast of local Indian dishes for a welcome dinner. I think they were disappointed, though they tried to hide it, that after I barely tasted two items, I was visibly sweating, and chugging my bottled water. After that, I ate a lot of *chapati, naan,* and *paratha.* The breads were delicious, and not as terrifyingly spicy as the Southern Indian dishes. I had to remember to only eat them with my right hand. I didn't want to gross out anyone at the table by using my left hand, the *toilet* hand. I also ate a lot of *aloo samosa*, hearty, deep-fried dough triangles filled with potatoes. I was embarrassed I could not eat and enjoy the local food, as the family was so thoughtful in introducing me to it.

After two days to shake off the jetlag, I started to adjust to Mangalore. At all times of the day and night, I heard the wind-up electric mixer sounds of motorbikes, men hollering in the street, and the shrieks of the black birds that would fight you for a crumb of your samosa. I often caught myself breathing through my mouth, so as not to inhale the thick odor of mud, garbage, and the sharp summertime sweat of more than 500,000 people packed together in a relatively small space. Mangalore was so different from where I lived, in the suburbs of Minneapolis. I was so curious about this place, the people, the traditions, the food. There was no way I would blend in, and I just tried to be respectful. India was not my country. I was a guest.

As part of the pre-wedding plans, Shruti's family hired a van and driver for a day of temple visits to offer *puja* (prayers), and ancestor visits to pay respect before the wedding. I was deeply honored to be included. I also had no idea what was happening. I should have done more research. This was definitely not something listed in the Frommer's or Fodor's guidebooks I bought. Maybe I should have demurred when they invited me because this was their tradition, not mine. But it was a conundrum. Would they be offended if I declined? Or were they just inviting me out of hospitality, out of obligation? I did not dwell on that.

    The morning of the pilgrimage, I got out of bed when it was still dark. I showered but was soon sweating again as the rattling AC unit in my hotel room only fitfully generated a trickle of cool air, and it seemed to have surrendered to the swampy August heat. I dressed in a kurta top, the one Shruti's mother instructed me to wear with my jeans: long, deep teal, short-sleeved, embellished with large and small red and gold metallic flowers. As I made my way to the small hotel lobby, I saw gray and pinkish light was just beginning to seep over the city. I waited, and after a couple of minutes, a dusty white van pulled up to the hotel entrance. The van door slid open, and Shruti hopped out, wearing a deep purple kurta top, a turquoise scarf, and jeans. Her long top was fitted and highly embellished with embroidery and sequins and showed her brown, thin arms. She shoved a paper cup full of warm liquid at me and said, *chai, slam it!* I did and followed her into the interior of the van.

    I settled on the bench seat between Shruti and her 8-year-old niece, who found me both entertaining and a great source of knowledge. She asked endless (endless) questions about my kids, my house, what kind of food I ate, why my skin was so white, and on and on. She inquired as only young children can – with curiosity, forthrightness, without filters. Every time I answered a question, she grinned and thought of another one.

The van was full - Shruti, her parents, her sister, brother-in-law, niece, and I were all wide awake, ready for the day. I saw several boxes in the back of the van that I assumed were filled with food for the road trip. I was wrong. We stopped at temples, one after another for hours, and at each stop, the boxes were opened, and flowers, drinks, and fruit offerings were pulled out. Each temple visit was an immersive experience that followed a specific structure. I followed the family. We rang the temple bell upon our arrival. We breathed in the day's floral offerings, sweet and fragrant, like entering an immense garden with only two types of flowers - marigolds and jasmine.

We lit skinny sticks of incense, and the family performed *puja* after carefully placing their offerings in front of statues of the gods, and sometimes lighting oil lamps. Many statues depicting gods were in shades of blue, green, and yellow. They looked very human-like. Shruti's father explained to me that they were supposed to look like humans, but also superior to humans since they had powers we humans do not. As there is no way we could comprehend God, these statues were an attempt to give the human mind a form of the formless Brahman (God).

Once the family finished their prayers, they received a special blessing from the temple priests and hoped for additional blessings from the gods. Most of the temples were packed with worshipers. The temples were awash in deep red and the yellow-gold of saffron. Each temple was covered in a heavy fog of incense and smelled of food in various stages of decay. One of our last temple stops was the Temple Pangala, with its silver walls and impressive representations of the gods. I bought postcards there, while the family received their blessings.

    The last stop of our very long day was at the home of Shruti's grandmother. It took us hours to get there. The van left the highway, and turned onto a smaller road, onto a dirt road, then onto what could generously be called a path. It was more like a suggestion of travel direction, a cleared space covered with sun-bleached dirt, large and small rocks, and thin ruts to follow. All the while we bounced in the van, straining the shocks, until we finally pulled into a small, dusty village. There hadn't been any road signs for a very long time.

    We slowly drove past cows and skinny chickens. Several women paused their chores to openly stare at us. The driver stopped the van in front of the brown squat structure that was Shruti's grandmother's house. We got out of the van and stretched, trying to work the kinks out of our necks and backs. We removed our shoes and entered the house. Shruti's father led the way. Her grandmother's house had several rooms, and was cool, compared to the blasting summer sun and pervasive humidity outside. The main room was only illuminated by the light streaming through a single window. Once my eyes adjusted to the dimness, I saw a tiny, white-haired woman perched on a red padded chair. She was flanked by two members of her staff, a man and a woman. They were referred to as her servants, and neither would look at me. As we walked toward Shruti's grandmother, she began to squint at me through her thick-lensed glasses. When we were nearly in front of her, her rheumy brown eyes opened wide, and she began saying a phrase, over and over, seemingly alarmed. She became agitated, and I looked at Shruti, horrified that I caused this elderly, slight woman such distress. I was very confused.

Her grandmother motioned Shruti over with her hand, no larger than a child's, bony, wizened by the years. Shruti put her hands together and murmured *Namaste*, and reached down and touched her grandmother's feet, as a sign of respect. Her grandmother grabbed her by the arm, tightly, and started talking in a papery, urgent voice. This went on for quite some time, with occasional glances and head nods at me. I stood stock-still, unsure of what sign of disrespect I had shown, and wondering if I could beg forgiveness in some way, so as not to ruin this special day. I thought I might cry. Finally, Shruti made her way back to me and translated the whole conversation.

In her advanced age, her grandmother had become fixated on death and spoke of it often. The night before our arrival, she had a dream in which she was told that a white ghost would be visiting her soon with a message. Then, ten hours later, the van pulled up, riled the dust and dirt in front of the house, and from the van emerged a white ghost – a woman with white hair, white skin, and blue eyes. She had never had a white person in her home in all her years, and she was very frightened. She was convinced that I was the ghost from her dream, and I had a death message for her. She was understandably upset.

I said, "Oh my god, Shruti, what should I do?" Shruti quickly consulted with her father, and they decided that to placate the old woman, I should, indeed deliver a message. They suggested something vague, in English, along the lines of, *I bring you a message. You needn't worry. You are a good woman. You have the favor of the gods.* I walked up to the old woman, placed my hands together, and said *Namaste*, with a deep bow of my head. I thought of my petite Irish grandmother, her lively blue eyes, her snowy white hair, and her unshakeable faith in God. I solemnly addressed Shruti's grandmother as I would have my grandmother. I slowly and deliberately delivered the message, maybe adding a few words, in English. Shruti translated, likely embellishing on what I had said. Her grandmother's eyes filled with tears, and relief washed over her small wrinkled face. I looked over at Shruti's father, and he gave me a small nod. It felt like we were able to release a collective breath.

The official pre-wedding visit commenced, and we were served tea and sweets by the servants. When the visit was over, I said to Shruti's grandmother in English, "Thank you for the honor of visiting your home."

When we stepped outside, we noticed that a small group of women and children, and a couple of men had gathered outside the home. When I came out of the house, the women stared and covered their mouths, whispering to each other. I smiled and waved at them, and the whispering became more intense. Several of the women shook their children and pointed at me. Once we got in the van and started bouncing down the uneven road, Shruti's father explained to me that there had never been a white person in that village. Never. The village had no electricity, and the villagers had no television, so they had never seen someone who looked like me. He said they were calling me the *ghost woman*. He smiled and said that my visit was a huge, unexpected event in the village, and the most exciting thing to happen there in decades. He and Shruti started laughing and said the people in the village would be talking about my visit, adding on details, true or not true, for years to come. I looked out the dirty van window, as we headed back to the city, and thought, *I'll be talking about this visit for years to come, too.*

    That long day in the van was illuminating, and I think back on it, once in a while. Shruti's grandmother was not so different than my grandmother, my great-grandmother. These women were deeply religious, and faithful, and worked hard to secure their virtuous spot in the unknown afterlife. They had a deep concern for their souls and tried their best to ensure they remained in the favor of their God/gods. They had earned their folded and furrowed faces. Their lives could not have been easy. These women deserved our respect, our support, and our efforts to make their last years comfortable and peaceful.

Over the years, I have thought a lot about that trip, the temples, and those rituals. They were not so different from what I experienced growing up Catholic. Our saints were our gods, our smoky incense released in swinging metal censors, by chanting priests. We prayed. We lit candles. We were blessed.

The Kidnapper

It was August in India. The air felt nearly gelatinous, and as I stepped outside, it enveloped me like a hot, moist rug. It was 2010, and I had been an honored guest at my friend Shruti's wedding. After five days of nonstop activities, the bride and groom left for their honeymoon, and I was going home to Minnesota. Shruti's father had booked me into a hotel on the outskirts of Bangalore, booked a driver to take me to the airport, and gave me the payment receipt, just in case of problems.

Shruti's brother-in-law dropped me off at the hotel in the early afternoon. The staff did not speak English, and everyone seemed immune to my few words of Hindi. I was frustrated, but it was my fault. I probably should have taken the time to learn more than please, thank you, hello, goodbye, yes, no, sorry, and how much. I had a lot of time to kill, so after I dropped my bags in my room, I left the hotel to buy some small gifts and take a last look around.

I made my way down the sidewalk, which was swamped with people, and dozens of skinny brown and white street dogs, expertly maneuvering around people's legs and sandal-clad feet. The street was awash with the angry buzz of motorbikes, construction sounds, yelling, and the reek of old deep-fried food and urine. After, mumbling sorry for the 20th time, as I was carried by the crowd and plowed into someone, I realized there was zero chance of me blending in. I was 5'10", with curly blonde hair, and blue eyes. Sturdy midwestern stock, generic and invisible in Minnesota. In my mind, I batted away echoes of advice from friends and guidebooks. Be very careful. Bring a man and don't venture out alone. Pay attention to the surroundings. Alarmists, I thought. Xenophobes, even. It was 2010, after all, and I had traveled solo around the world mostly with no issues. I maintained that people are basically good.

Every shop owner was trying to make a sale that day, and each loudly implored me to come into their shop – lady! Best stuff, cheap! Some followed me down the sidewalk, yelling their best sales pitch, and eventually, I stopped smiling and stared straight ahead as I walked. It was exhausting. I ventured into a few tiny shops, looking for those staffed by women, and bought my presents. Jewel-toned little purses with sequins and bells. Elephant carvings. Dangling golden earrings, and packets of clinking bangles.

With my shopping complete, and an arm full of plastic bags, I had no desire to walk back to the hotel in the spongy heat. I flagged down the nearest tuk-tuk, and the driver and I agreed on a price. It was only after I realized we had gone around the same block three times that I told him to stop. The driver then demanded an exorbitant amount of money, more than ten times what we had agreed on to get to the hotel. He hopped out of the tuk-tuk and began to holler and wave his arms. People stared. I stood firm and finally just handed over the agreed-upon rupees, and started to push my way out of the tuk-tuk. He blocked me, and his coffee-colored face was so close to mine that spit droplets flew out of his mouth and landed on my sweaty cheek, as he continued his tirade. He then tried to snatch the packages out of my hands. I yanked them away, shoved past him, and melted into the noisy crowd on the street.

I thought to myself how "lucky" I was to be tall and strong, though I did look over my shoulder for the rest of the long, hot walk. Maybe my friends, including Shruti, and the guidebooks were right. Maybe India was not an especially safe place for a woman traveling alone. The rest of my trip had been so great, the people so warm and gracious, I didn't want to think about that. I was leaving the country in a few hours.

Back at the hotel, I was getting ready to shower and change my clothes for the flight, when I heard a scuffling in the hallway, like the skittering of an animal in an attic. I looked over and noticed a large gap between the bottom of the wooden door and the floor. In that space, I could see shadows moving. I strode over, got down on my hands and knees, and looked through the gap. Bookended on either side of the door frame, were disembodied dark brown eyes, each with long lashes, and a slice of brown nose, staring back at me.

I scrambled up and yelled, "Leave me alone!" As I went to the bathroom to get a thin bath towel to shove in the gap, I thought, holy shit, what is happening? What is wrong with these guys?

I shoved the towel into the space between the door and

the tile floor. After the tuk-tuk incident, and now this, I felt a little anxious. But I was also starting to fume. Angry and indignant thoughts tumbled over each other in my head. What was it about these men, maybe this country, I mused, that made it acceptable to treat women like this? I huffed it was not okay. I double-checked the lock on the door, and dragged the flimsy wooden dresser that smelled of mildew, in front of the door. I hurried to the bathroom to take a shower. I left the shower curtain open and set two drinking glasses next to the sink. If someone got into my room, I wanted to see them and have a way to fight back.

At 11:45pm, I went down to the hotel lobby, with my small suitcase and red backpack, and waited for my car. The chain-smoking man behind the registration desk chain stared at me. At 12:10am, I walked over to him and asked in English, slowly and clearly, if he had seen my driver. He smirked and pretended he didn't know what I was saying.

Eventually, he sauntered across the lobby, swung open the grubby glass door, leaned out, and said something to another man.

He came back into the lobby and said "Hurry! Hurry! Hurry! You have to go now!"

I grabbed my two pieces of luggage, struggled to get through the single-door frame, and walked toward a dark car that had just pulled up to the curb. The driver wore a faded yellow dress shirt, and he hefted my suitcase in the trunk. I held my backpack in front of me and got into the backseat of the car. As soon as I sat, I was surrounded by the smell of food grease, hair oil, and body odor.

We pulled out on the highway and headed toward the airport, which was about thirty minutes away. At first, I tried to be friendly, making polite chitchat about the weather, and about how tasty the Indian food was. When I mentioned that it was much hotter than the food I ate at home, the driver chuckled. Eventually, I ran out of things to say, and for a long time, it was quiet in the car. It was late. The windows were up, it was hot in the thick darkness, and I felt a little drowsy.

Then the driver cleared his throat and spoke, or rather, started drilling me with questions, one after another. At first, I thought he was just curious about who I was, and what it was like where I lived. Then the type of questions, the cadence, and his tone of voice changed. My radar went off. It jerked me out of my sleepiness. I could see his eyes watching me in the rearview mirror.

He asked, "What does your husband do for a job? He must be very important. What is his education? How big is your house? How many cars do you have?"

I wanted to downplay my status, so I said, "My husband works in a factory, we live in a small apartment, and we only have one old car." I forced a self-deprecating chuckle.

I could feel the tension building in the car, like bread rising too fast. There was silence, but it was heavy and loaded.

And then he said, "Your bag is very small, madam. I see you did not buy many things. You should purchase more gifts for your family. I will take you to my cousin's store – it won't take long."

"Where is this store?" I asked.

He pointed vaguely to the left of the highway, where I could see nothing but inky darkness, outlines of vegetation, and unlit dirt streets. My gut, my brain, and everything I had ordered me to prepare. Fight back.

I politely said, "No, thank you." He tapped the brakes and started slowing the car. Then I said it again, more forcefully. He eased off the highway, moving toward the left turn lane and I felt an anchor of fear drop in my chest. My heart rate quickened, every beat pounding in my ears. But I pushed past the terror. I had to.

I said, "My friend's father knows who you are! He is an important businessman in Bangalore!"

The driver continued slowing.

I yelled, "My friends are waiting for me at the airport, and I told them what you and your car look like."

I had a mobile phone, with no international minutes left, and no service outside the city center. But I hoped he didn't realize that. I waved my useless phone at him. He flipped on his turn signal with a small clunk. I took a breath and screamed at the back of his head, with as much force and volume as I could muster, while pummeling the back of his seat with my feet, and my knees, hard.

"Take me to the airport, goddamnit! Take me there now! Now!" I shrieked at him until I was hoarse.

Sweat coated my body in that swampy car, with its AC

pushing out a sad dribble of cool air. Pieces of hair stuck to my forehead, and I balled my hands into tight, fighting fists. I could see the faint glow of the lights at the airport ahead. I thought maybe I could jump out and run down the highway. Losing my suitcase would be better than getting murdered, or worse. I tried to calculate how fast the driver was moving, and whether I could tumble out without a serious injury. I continued to kick and knee him in the back and tried to hit him in the back of the head with my elbows.

I was afraid to get too close because I didn't want him to grab my hands, my arms, my hair.

Finally, he stopped the car on the side of the road. We sat there for a protracted, meaningful, pivotal moment. My life could head in one direction, toward the light of the airport, toward the goodness of home. Or the other direction, down that dark dirt road and what came after. What would surely come after. I know that driver could hear every wheezy, ragged breath I was taking. He met my eyes in the rearview mirror, then looked away as he signaled right, and slowly pulled back on the highway.

We rode in edgy silence the rest of the way to the airport. The car was still filled with that thick tension, although I believed the worst had passed. The driver pulled up to the entrance of the airport to drop me off. The area was flooded with artificial brightness and teemed with life, energy, and people. Witnesses. As we neared the terminal, I could see police officers guarding the glass airport entrance doors. I noticed other passengers showed their paper tickets and boarding passes to the guards before being allowed in. I yanked my documents from my backpack.

As soon as the car stopped, I shoved my door open, peeled myself off the damp vinyl seat, and leaped out. I stalked to the trunk to retrieve my suitcase. The driver got out of the car, followed me closely, and lifted out my case. I snatched it from him. The driver looked around and then started hollering at me, maybe in Hindi, maybe not. Like a snake striking, he reached out and grabbed my arm, hard, and his long and bony brown fingers dug into my flesh.

I wrested away my arm and ran. I held my red backpack under my arm and pulled my suitcase clattering behind me, toward the airport entrance.

As I reached the entrance, a guard stopped me, and said, "Pass. Pass." It took me a second to realize he wanted to see my ticket, and I held it up.

The driver had caught up to me and continued to scream and shake his fist at me, standing just a few feet away. I could see his furious, wild eyes, and was close enough that I could smell onions on his breath.

I lurched toward the glass doors, to safety, and the guard blocked my way. He said calmly, 'You did not pay. You must pay. Must pay driver."

With panic in my voice, I said, "I paid. My friend's father paid. I have a paper that says it was paid. Please, please let me in.

Please! This driver is a bad man, and he tried to hurt me, please. PLEASE let me in!"

The guard looked at me coolly and flicked his eyes toward the driver, who continued to complain and waved his skinny fist toward me.

I wailed to the guard. "Please let me in!" as I waved my ticket.

He gave me a tiny nod and moved aside. I launched myself toward the glass door, the driver's protestations still battering my ears. I pounded on the still-closed door with the heels of my hands. It finally opened with a swoosh. I stumbled into the building, pulling my suitcase so hard it tipped over, and I heard the door click closed behind me. Coolness. Safety. My legs shook so badly, I had to lean against a wall to stay upright.

I had made it.

There was still sweat dripping down my temples when I got to the front of the queue at the check-in counter. My hands quivered from the surge of adrenaline as I handed over my ticket and my passport, and numbly answered the agent's questions. I had to repeat my birthdate twice, as it came out garbled the first time she asked me. At the first stand I saw, I pulled some rupees from the bottom of my backpack and bought a bottle of water. My mouth was dry and sticky, and my throat felt abraded from all the screaming. The room-temperature water was delicious. I stood for a moment, enjoying the sensation of the water coating my throat, like a salve.

I followed the signs to security, where I was told to stand behind a red line on the floor. I clutched the bottle of water, forgetting I would have to throw it away. The back of my cotton polo shirt was still damp, and flop sweat rolled down my ribs. After several minutes, a uniformed female security attendant took me to a small booth. She reached over and pulled the heavy red curtain closed. I was told to set down my backpack and stand on the short round wooden platform. She then instructed me to take off my clothes except for my bra and underwear. I was shocked and did as I was told. I stood stock-still on that wooden platform while dry, brown, unfamiliar hands slid over my skin, my bra, and my underwear. It was awful. A small cry caught in my throat.

My arms began to shake, my teeth chattered, and not just from the humiliation of standing on a platform in the Bangalore airport, in front of a stranger, in my underwear, like a criminal, a terrorist. My body was catching up to the car ride to the airport, the tuk-tuk, the eyes under the hotel room door. All of it. My nose ran, and I didn't care. The attendant seemed confused about why I was crying. She said I could have my water. I didn't want the water. I just wanted to go home. I wanted to be home, where my decisions, my body were my own.

On the plane, I didn't sleep. I thought about that driver, that car, that dirt road. The beads that swayed below the rearview mirror. The creaking when I moved on the vinyl seat. Was that even the driver Shruti's father had hired? I never told Shruti what happened. I'm not sure if it was from embarrassment, shame, or out of respect for our friendship or her father.

Nine years later, I read about a young woman suffering a horrific attack on a bus in Delhi, and later dying from her injuries. While that could have happened anywhere, I found myself holding my breath as I read. What happened to her was horrendous - more violent, more sexual, more grave than what I experienced, yet I felt a small amount of kinship with her. I pursed my lips to stop them from trembling. I was there once again, that night, the heat, the car. The terror of not knowing what was going to happen. The desperation. My fate in the hands of a stranger, of a man. Why does this type of violence keep happening? Why is this somehow okay? Why can't someone stop these men and hold them accountable? Women are not garbage. I tried my best not to hyperventilate. Breathe in. Breathe out. I said a prayer for that young woman. Then I said a prayer for myself, in relief, in gratitude.

RANGE LIGHTS

A pair of lights used to help ships navigate
through dangerous or shallow water.

Haleakala Blues

The gas gauge had been urgently dinging for the last twelve miles, as we drove switchback after switchback working our way to the summit of Haleakala on the island of Maui. The gauge was pegged in the E zone, and that damn bell was urgently (urgently!) warning us we would soon run out of gas. My brother, Tim was driving the shiny black Dodge Charger rental, and while his face registered no alarm, he has a poker face that would fit in on Easter Island. I was having a meltdown.

We ended up on Maui for Christmas because Hurricane Ian had thwarted our original plans to go to Florida. The three of us - Tim, my husband Steven, and I, were fortunate that we had been able, on short notice, to rebook for Hawaii. I had thought, wow the travel gods are looking out for us. I can almost laugh about that now. Almost.

We arrived on Maui without incident. I surprised Steven with tickets to Pearl Harbor, so the Monday before Christmas, we arrived for our sunrise, 30-minute flight to Honolulu. They didn't even serve coffee. It felt very strange to get on a flight with only a 12x12 inch clear purse, the only type they allowed at Pearl Harbor. I'm usually a "mom purse" traveler– snacks, first aid kit, multiple pens, notebook, Kleenex, lipstick, mints, sunscreen, chargers. I felt naked. At Pearl Harbor, it was rainy and windy. The terrible weather broke just long enough for us to ride the 1:00pm boat out to the

Pearl Harbor Memorial. It felt eerily quiet and heavy with sorrow, as we stood above the USS Arizona. Fuel slowly seeps from the ship, after some 80 years, still creating small slicks and rainbows on the gray water.

After the tour, we went back to the Honolulu airport and enjoyed a nice long lunch in the only sit-down restaurant we could find, before our flight back to Maui. We were supposed to be home by dinner. Then, over the next twelve hours, most of which we spent locked inside the terminal, I got a notification and another and another that our 5:00pm flight was delayed. First thirty minutes, then an hour, three hours, five hours, seven hours. Around 1:00 am, there was nearly a low-key riot in the terminal, as there was no food, drinks, or blankets available to us, and people were cold and hungry. Babies were crying. Hawaiian Airlines finally canceled the flight at 1:30am. Five hours later, somewhat miraculously we were on a Southwest flight, headed back to Maui. By the time we arrived, it had been a very, very long 27 hours, which was supposed to be, much like Gilligan's Island, a three-hour tour.

The next day, Wednesday, dawned sunny and gorgeous, the type of Maui day you see in stock photos. We decided to drive up to the summit of Haleakala. We had been there several years before, but it was so foggy and misty, we couldn't see ten feet in front of us. We laughed whenever we looked at the pictures because all you could see was us bundled up in layers, with a solid white cloudbank behind us.

We paid our national park fee and drove into the park itself.

We saw ominous brown signs posted one after another, warning us of the treacherous nature of the summit above – there was no food available, there were no medical facilities, and there were no gas stations. I leaned over to see how much gas we had, and Tim said we had a range of more than 100 miles. "We're just fine," he said. We had sandwiches and drinks in the backseat, so we were prepared and ready to start the drive up to the summit. I saw sign after sign that said to watch out for Nene birds, and I tried to Google them. I had no cell service, and I gave up.

As we followed the road up and up, the views of the valleys and the ocean were spectacular. When we reached about 3,500 feet, I looked over and noticed that our fuel was burning at an alarming pace. I mean, it was burning fast. I can almost hear it ticking down toward empty, I thought. Holy crap. I said to Tim, "Our gas is going down quick – are you worried?" He responded with his typical, droll, "Nah, it's fine." We kept driving. Clumps of cyclists came flying down the mountain in their matching rental helmets, and tourist buses and vans continuously rumbled up and cruised down in low gear. I spotted the Visitor's Center parking lot at 7,000 feet with relief, and said, "Oh great, we can turn around." Tim said, "Nope, we're fine. We're going to the top." We kept driving. My anxiety clicked up a notch every time the fuel gauge clicked down another marker toward E. I stared straight ahead, trying to take photos through the windshield, thinking, at least I could document where we bit the dust. There were no shoulders for long stretches of the road. Then, with twelve miles of switchbacks in front of us to reach the summit, the countdown to the beginning of the end of our gas started in earnest. The low-fuel yellow light came on. It was not a relief. Then, the gas alarm on the controls started dinging, clanging like a ship going down in the night.

My eyes were transfixed by the controls, by the gauges. I wanted to focus on the scenery – a hundred shades of green, V-shaped hills and deep cut valleys, outcroppings of black volcanic rock, all leading to the blue, blue ocean, but I couldn't do it. I couldn't tear my eyes away from the dash. I looked at my phone, over and over, and I had no service. I was a live wire, throwing off the tense vibrations that only extreme anxiety can generate, and only those with anxiety can understand.

A few switchbacks later, it happened. The gauge tipped over and pegged solid red at E. Then it gave up completely and fell below E. In my head, I was running through all possible scenarios, many of which ended with an alarming Thelma & Louise-type of unscripted demise. AAA would not come to rescue us. Our phones didn't work, even if we wanted to call someone to help. What if the car stalled in the middle of a switchback? What if one of those barreling buses hit us? What if, what if, what if. I shared my concerns with the guys, and by the way they were staring at me, I could tell they thought I was a little unhinged. Being silly. They started talking to me in low, soothing tones. Especially Steven. Patronizing. That thing, a muscle maybe, that kept my tears tucked in my eyes was just about ready to give way.

In that car, on that beautiful Maui day, my fear tripped the switch, which unexpectedly sent me back to the car ride in India. The kidnapping. To the truck crossing the bridge from Wisconsin after the assault. To helplessness, to sweating, to the unknown.
It felt awful, and I struggled to be present. I tried to focus on my breathing. The last thing I wanted was a panic attack and to show my true colors to Tim and Steven. My weakness. My inability to control my mind, and my emotions. There were so many things swirling in my brain, that I could not grab one thought and hang on to it. In those horrible minutes, I felt alone, even though I was in the car with two of the men I trusted with my life. I thought, is this the way it's always going to be?

But wait, I thought. Just wait. I tried to pause before I crumpled, before I dissolved like meringue touching water. Why did I feel…sucker-punched? Undone. Some soft, vulnerable part of my past was activated and twitched. All those conversations. All those men. A lifetime of them. All those times I was told I was too emotional. Being told, stop talking back. Being told, children are to be seen, not heard. Those nights driving across the desert, when I thought I was in love, nights with fresh bruises swelling on my cheek, my neck, that I deserved for being stupid. The smirk on my grandfather's leathered face when he told me no one would believe you. All those memories competed for space in my mind. My terror started giving way to an indignant rage. Fury. This time I was going to give them a piece of my mind. This time.

Then, Tim pointed to the sign that said the summit was less than a mile away, and I was distracted from the speech I had started to rehearse in my head. I flipped back to thinking about the worst-case scenarios. Would we make it to the top? I thought about praying, but I think I've cried wolf a few too many times over the years to be taken seriously by a higher power.

I watched the odometer. I held my breath as I waited for each tenth-mile number to drop into place, each getting us closer to the top. And then we were there, in the parking lot, a big, flat, windblown space at the top of the volcano mountain. I spotted the first available parking spot and when Tim didn't take it, I groused as he drove around, looking for a place with a good view, or at least out of the wind. I was listening closely for the sputtering, knocking sound that would signal we had drained the last ounce of fuel. It didn't come. We got out of the car, put on jackets and hats, and started to walk. It was a clear day, but very cold, with a wind chill in the upper 30s, as we walked around and took a few photos, and I continued to fret. I could not wait to get back to the car. Or maybe I could. I was, as Steven would say, 100% wrapped around my own axel. I felt ashamed and embarrassed at how I was acting, and I felt helpless as I drowned in a soup of anxious thoughts. I tried to be my own voice of reason – nothing terrible is going to happen. Someone will help us if we need it. But my anxiety yelled in both ears, and I was unable to hear anything else. I wanted to have fun, have an adventure, create a great story, but I could not do it. And that made me angry. I thought, and not for the first time that day, sometimes it sucks to be me.

Remember the old question of which weighs more – a pound of bricks or a pound of feathers? That day I was holding and balancing a pound, or ten pounds, or 100 pounds of anxious feathers, and I was suffocating and collapsing under the weight.

After taking a few laps around the observation area, heads down to the wind, we went back to the car, and Tim started the engine. It roared to life. One feather lifted off. The warning bell was still dinging, but I tried to block it out. We made our way through the parking area, littered with vans, buses, small children, dogs, and bicycles. Tim put the car in neutral, and we started to descend. Another feather took flight. By the time we got down to the Visitor's Center, the gas gauge had ticked back up to just above E. For the first time in my life, I was thrilled to see the fuel gauge hit E, this time from the other side. We stopped and ate our sandwiches and chips. As we coasted down through switchback after switchback, the altitude decreased and the air pressure increased, and drop by drop, the gas expanded and pushed the gauge up, slowly, slowly. By the time we neared the park exit, the reading was just below a quarter tank.

The guys could not resist poking at me, now that the danger had passed, and there were comments made about how Tim magically made gasoline as we were coming down. About how physics works. I felt dumb, stung by their teasing, but that was arguably better than the crushing anxiety I had felt at the top. Better than the rage. While I know my husband and my brother both love me, sometimes they are insensitive. Their teasing often has a hard edge to it, and rather than landing softly, as teasing should, sometimes those hidden darts hit me right in my soft, insecure underbelly. I deflate into feelings of being inadequate, not smart enough, feeling ditzy and spacy. I'm sure their intention is never to wound me, but it happens, and each time, it strains the thin cable of trust I have with them. It makes it just a little harder not to pull away. To retract. I have to fight the urge to add another layer to my armor. Maybe sometime I'll tell them that. Maybe I won't.

As Tim signaled his turn out of the park, I finally had cell service, and I Googled "gas stations near me." I could breathe. The rest of the feathers took flight, sprinkling the roadside as we turned onto the highway.

Dayton is Not An Uber Town

I should have known. Truly, I should have. There were only the cheapest Uber X cars available, and the nearest one was 13 minutes away. The last Uber I had taken in Dayton, Ohio, was the year before and the whole car smelled like old pizza and cats. But I was committed, and we needed to get to Cincinnati, to the airport. And we needed to get there, fast.

I stood on the cold sidewalk, alongside my boss, Karen: a tiny, aggressive, demanding woman, all of which she was perfectly well aware of, and unapologetic for. Every two minutes, she asked me when the car was coming. To save money and get direct flights, we were driving from Dayton to Cincinnati, and then she was flying home to Connecticut, and I was flying home to Minnesota. It had been a long few days. The Uber could not arrive soon enough.

When the car arrived, I had to double-check the app. The image on my phone was more of a representative sample, rather than an actual photo of the vehicle in front of us. This car had seen some hard living; There were several crunched-in dents, and a deep crack traversing the windshield. I looked at Karen and shrugged. The driver stopped the small SUV, hopped out, opened the back hatch, and started piling up dirty softball bats, gym bags, and dozens of softballs. *Sorry,* he mumbled. He shoved the equipment over far enough so that Karen's small suitcase and mine could wedge in.

We climbed into the back of that Toyota RAV 4, and I delicately nudged half-empty Gatorade bottles with my foot. There was a wet dog smell in the car or something else equally organic. We put on our seatbelts, and our driver, named Keith, according to Uber, pulled out on the road. We had made it about three minutes down the highway, when Keith hollered back to us, "Hey! Do you know how far it is to the airport?"

Karen and I exchanged looks. Keith told us that his phone had died. Keith said he couldn't use the Uber app. He couldn't get directions to the airport. I offered him my Apple charger, but his phone was an Android, so it was of zero value. I told Keith that I thought it was about an hour to the Cincinnati airport.

Keith looked up, in the rearview mirror, eyes wide. "Wait? Where are you going again?" We told him Cincinnati, and he looked like he was going to hyperventilate, and his hands started drumming against the steering wheel. He launched into a sad, sad, and progressively less believable story about how it was his first day as an Uber driver, and he was short of cash, that his girlfriend had taken his wallet that morning.

I asked him how much gas he had, and he said, "Well, near as I can tell, about a tenth of a tank. It's gonna start dinging pretty soon." I said, "We need to get to the airport, Keith, so why don't you exit, I'll give you your tip money, and you can fill up your tank. And you can pick up a charger while you're there."

Keith took the next exit, found a BP station, and pulled in as the gas gauge bell started to go off. It was going to be a long trip, so I gave Keith twenty dollars, hoping that was enough to get us to Cincinnati. Keith went into the station and was gone for what seemed like a very long time just to pay the attendant. He came out, filled up the tank, and apologized for the wait. "Bathroom," he said. "No chargers."

We got back on the road. My phone was charged, and I told Keith I would navigate us. Within the first few minutes, I could sense something was wrong. Very wrong. Keith was no longer drumming the steering wheel in that nervy cadence. Quite the opposite. He now looked half asleep, slack-mouthed, and the car was gently swaying across our lane, and into the lanes adjacent.

Without raising my voice, I said, "Hey, Keith. Why don't you crank up the radio? Why don't you tell us a little about Dayton, and you? How about if you put the window down?" It was January in Ohio, and I knew we were going to freeze, but better than having Keith asleep at the wheel. I kept him talking for 50 miles down I-71 and I-75. Karen studiously looked at her phone, but stole glances at me and raised her eyebrows. Neither of us could feel our hands. I peppered Keith with questions, hoping each answer would be less slurred than the last.

Karen didn't know this, but despite the chill, I was sweating. I was in the back seat of that RAV-4 in Ohio, but I was also in the back seat of that sedan in India. I was fighting the grip of panic. When Keith exited the highway, I flashed back to the highway in India, in the dark, waiting for the driver to decide to rape me, kill me, turn me over to his friends, or let me go. I was again trying to get to the airport, to protection, not knowing if I was going to make it or not. My heart was pounding, but somehow, miraculously, I found calm. I dug deep and found the ability to manage Keith and, in doing that, control the situation, and create my own safety. Protect myself (and Karen). Get us to the airport.

Finally, we saw the sign for the Cincinnati airport. I thanked the universe for getting us that far. Keith pulled up to the terminal, and we raced around the car to get our bags. Karen and I hightailed it into the airport. As we headed toward security, I realized my hands were shaking, and not from the cold.

Karen said, "I can't BELIEVE how you kept so calm, kept him talking. I was ready for him to leave us on the side of the freeway!"

"Lots of practice," I replied. As I put my bag into the security scanner, I thought about how many times over the years I had to be calm: I survived assaults, neglect, and other traumas. I lived through a childhood of alcoholic parents, a series of abusive partners, and a mentally ill daughter who later struggled with opioid addiction. I held it together. I never gave up. Practice? It was second nature. No one was better at it than me. I understood in my bones that my survival hinged on calmness. Getting upset was for other people.

TRANSIT

Whippin' Shitties

My father was one of those drivers who is inexplicably drawn to every lumpy, muddy, or water-based obstacle along the side of any road. Once behind the wheel, he was eagle-eyed at spotting every rippling puddle, grainy gray snow pile, or slag of mud. Soon, one front tire was rolling over or into that road fudge, or if he was lucky, two tires, and a bonus if he could fly off the stuff with a bounce. Without regard to the clearance of the undercarriage, the state of the tires, the newness of the vehicle, or the fact that he washed it the day before, he, and by default, the car, was drawn to these watery, slippery Sirens. Maybe it was a biological imperative for him, like building a fire or correcting my math. Or perhaps it was from his childhood, summers spent at the ranch in Nebraska, driving tractors and trucks with little instruction and even less supervision.

In the 1970s my father bought a brand-new gold Subaru. He may have named it, or maybe not. It was a sturdy, practical, little tank-like vehicle, perfect for Minnesota winters, and safely toting around two kids. Unlike their blue Volkswagen bus, this was my parents' first car with four-wheel drive. The bus was driven to Alaska, on the new Yukon Highway, and sold to my relatives in Anchorage.

In our small-town neighborhood, buying a new car

was a happening. People talked. Rather, the men talked. Our neighborhood wasn't the kind of place where people splashed out on new things, especially a brand-new car. The families on our street had what we needed, and that was enough. It had to be enough because there wasn't much to spare at the end of the month. Most folks were getting by, with jobs like teaching school, construction, or working at the shoe factory. Our next-door neighbor, Tony, would sometimes offer us the nearly expired Hostess Dingdongs and Snowballs he pulled from the vending machines on his route, and we were delighted. So, something this extravagant, a new car, was newsworthy. When the weather warmed, we knew the guys in the neighborhood would casually stroll over to the driveway if someone was outside, especially washing the car, "I was just gettin' the mail, ya know," to check things out. Or they stopped their vehicle in front of the driveway, cranked down their window, and it would go something like this: "Hey, Mike, I see you got yourself one of those Sue-bar-roos. Did ya get a good deal? How's the mileage, what with gas prices? How's she drive?"

    Despite crackling cold, and gray clouds full of snow, the day my father was set to pick up the Subaru and drive it home was filled with buzzing anticipation, and I could barely control my excitement. My mother was going to drop the two of us at the dealership, and I was going to drive home with my father, in the new car. In the front seat. Just us two. I was eleven, and it was a banner day.

Before we left the dealership lot, he proudly pointed out all the features this car offered. He showed me how to turn on the wipers, the high beams, the defroster, and how to pull the emergency brake. He showed me the manual tucked in the glovebox, and where to enter the maintenance records. This was a half-dozen years before I would learn to drive, but it felt important to pay attention, and I listened.

As we exited the highway and drove up the hill to our street, my father looked proud and happy – something we rarely saw. My father had lived a tough life, filled with poverty, illness, and hard work. He suffered from chronic leg pain, stemming from a horrific car accident at fifteen, and a skin graft that never healed. He didn't often show his teeth, which were held together with scaffolding of bridges, gold fillings, and partials. My father was an introvert who loathed being the center of attention. He was a determined man, filled with grit and tenacity, nearly obsessed with creating a better life for himself and his family. We saw that tough side of him far more often than the pleased man he was that cold day.

As we crested the hill onto our street, my father smiled, showing all his teeth, and said let's take 'er for a ride. I thought he meant a quick drive around the quarter-mile loop of our street, which we called The Circle. The middle of The Circle was The Park, filled with well-maintained grass and a modest play structure. In the winter, the city cleared and leveled an area in the middle of The Park, banked it, flooded it, and transformed it into our neighborhood ice rink. Maybe my father would go fast around The Circle, which he had done before, really opened 'er up, which was both thrilling and frightening. None of our vehicles were ever built for speed or performance, but he pushed them to the brink, grinning like he was the king of NASCAR.

No, on that frosty day, my father had a different idea. He first drove slowly down the street toward our house, and then, rather than turn left into our driveway, he cranked the wheel to the right, revved the Subaru, and gunned it toward the low snowbank that surrounded the skating rink. The rink was glowing white with layers of city water ice, and smooth. I held my breath. I remember barely clearing that snow bank and the curb underneath, and my father launched the Subaru onto the ice rink. He stomped on the gas, slammed on the brakes, and spun the car in circles. Fast. This, I found out, was called whippin' shitties, or polite company calls it spinning donuts, but I guess we were not polite company. My father was having a blast out on the rink in his shiny new car, letting out the occasional, *woo!*, and I held tightly to the seatbelt across my chest, convinced, as I usually was, that something terrible was going to happen.

And it did. As my father hit yet another 360 spin he looked up and saw my mother standing in the picture window in our living room. Her arms were crossed, and even from that distance, we could tell she was pissed. My father made a couple more half-hearted rotations, and the joy seeped from him. He pointed the Subaru toward our driveway, gunned it once more, went back over the snow bank, and prepared for an extended tongue-lashing, followed by a full day of the silent treatment. I never got a chance to ask him, but I bet it was worth it.

When I took driver's ed years later in high school, there was a day when freezing rain had lacquered every surface with a shiny coat of ice. It was not safe for us trainees to be out on the street, especially since we had minimal instruction, and were only somewhat competent drivers. Our driving instructor, Mr. Woods, didn't cancel our lesson and met us in the high school parking lot. He, my driving partner Jon, and I, carefully shuffle-stepped to our clunky and practical driver's ed car. Mr. Woods took the wheel, warning us to buckle up. He eased out to the flattest part of the asphalt parking lot. Without warning, he hit the accelerator and then stomped the brakes. It felt like flying, like a tilt-o-whirl, like gravity was an afterthought. My teeth smacked together, and I didn't mind.

After a few more cycles of hitting the gas/brake, he slid the car to a stop. "You live in Minnesota, ya gotta know how to drive on ice." He told us it was time for practice, and my stomach knotted. I got out, came around the car, and slid into the driver's seat. Mr. Woods instructed me on the steps to take, and I gamely pushed on the gas pedal, then lightly tapped the brakes to a smooth, sliding stop.

Rolling his eyes, Mr. Woods told me to really hit the gas, and I did. He had the "Jesus take the wheel" brake pedal on his side, and he slammed it down. Hard. We pirouetted like the car was weightless. I tried it several more times, and by the end, I was smiling. No, I was grinning, showing all my teeth. I remembered that day on the ice rink with my father and I finally knew what he felt. Joy. Lightness. Freedom.

Driving Lessons

I come from car people – mechanics, drivers, tinkerers, and racers, going back generations. By car people, I mean men. My mother liked to cruise around town in her convertible, and my Aunt Karen enjoyed a good, cross-country road trip, but by and large, this was the domain of men.

In my family, we name our vehicles, sometimes affectionately, sometimes ironically: Maybelline, Trixie, Nancy Drew, Bertt, The Gray Goose, and Tommy Truck. As a teenage rite of passage, my parents bought me my first car, which I got to name. I called it Torque, which my 15-year-old self had thought was clever. Torque is what causes an object to rotate around an axis. Torque was quickly shortened to Tork because no one could remember how to spell it. Tork was a new-to-me, six-year-old 1976 Plymouth Duster. It was big and muscular in a beaky way, like an elongated and angular emu. The car had previously been owned by Mrs. Willis, who taught me math at St. Joseph Catholic School as Miss Campbell, and before that, she was Sister Marion. None of these Marions would be expected to drive a car marketed as a performance vehicle, with a beefy slant six engine and throaty pipes.

Tork's glossy, honey-brown paint job with tiny sparkles twinkled like carbonation in the sun. It was sturdy like a Detroit tank, heavy and roadworthy. Tork could hold six high school girls, our portal for giggling, gossip, and fruit-flavored lip gloss, and it took no offense at our half-screaming Journey and REO Speedwagon lyrics. But that all came later. After I proved to my father and the State of Minnesota I was fit and able to operate a vehicle.

When I was fifteen-almost-sixteen, my father "taught" me to drive The Duster, which he called my car. Never Tork. Always The Duster. I didn't argue.

The journey from rider to driver was slow and arduous, especially for an impatient fifteen-year-old, and it took months before I checked all the pre-driving boxes. I dutifully studied the Minnesota Driving Manual. I passed my permit test. I signed up for school-sponsored driver's ed, using my babysitting money. Our high school had a surprisingly robust driver's ed program, for a small town. We learned to drive in a fleet of blue, boxy 1980s-era Chrysler K-Cars. Each driver's ed car was kitted with a passenger-side brake pedal and was assigned to one instructor and two student drivers. Mr. Woods, the 10th-grade science teacher, would be my instructor. And then I found out my student driving partner was Jon, one of the most popular boys at my high school. He was gorgeous in a preppy, Breakfast Club or Sixteen Candles way. Blond hair that swooped, charmingly over his forehead. The most adorable dimples. Pastel Lacoste polo shirts with the collar always popped. Star player on the tennis team. In short, he was dreamy. And, far, far out of my league. I was doomed to watch and admire him, longingly, from a distance. I was a marching band/speech team/theater nerd, decades before being a nerd was cool, and the social lines in my high school were tightly drawn.

Despite looking like a happy extrovert, I was suffering. I had stuffed down all those years of abuse at the hands of my grandfather and my parents' insurance agent, coupled with poor behavior at the hands of the few boys I had dated. I had a full-blown eating disorder, which at the time I thought was a quest to get skinny and look good, but I now know was an attempt to make myself as small as possible to avoid standing out. Invisible people can't be victims. And, at long last, I felt in control, and that was more delicious than any food. Even though I was outwardly a successful student, my self-esteem was incredibly low, and any confidence I exuded felt like a lie. This was before we knew the term, imposter syndrome.

To say I was nervous when I showed up for lesson number one is the understatement of all understatements. I wore extra deodorant and my cutest Gloria Vanderbilt jeans.

When Jon and I arrived at the parking lot by the tennis courts after school, Mr. Woods was leaning on our freshly washed K-Car, smoking a cigarette. He looked every bit the laid-back dude he was. His straight salt and pepper hair was worn just a little long, resting on his collar, parted on one side, and flipped to the other. The perfect layers of feathering looked suspiciously hair-sprayed. He got his hair styled in a salon, not the barbershop. That was a thing, in our small town. People talked. Mr. Woods was a slender man, prone to wearing khaki pants, crewneck sweaters, and loafers. He was perpetually tan from the golf course and winter trips to Mexico. He was quick with a smile and deadly with a snappy comeback to the smart-asses in class. Students loved him.

When he saw Jon and me, he opened the passenger door and slipped into the seat. Then in one synchronized motion, he jerked the car door closed and pulled down his seatbelt, like he had probably done a hundred, or maybe a thousand times before. Even though he was probably Lutheran, I wonder if he said a little prayer to the patron saint of driver's ed teachers. We all needed whatever help we could muster.

Mr. Woods cranked down his window, and yelled, "Gilmore! You're up!" He kept his window rolled down and chain-smoked during that lesson, and every single one after that. The air carried the rubber band snap of Minnesota almost-spring, the kind that tickles your ears and makes your nose run just a little. After that lesson, we learned to bundle up.

When I heard my name that day, I walked up to the car, slowly opened the driver's side door, and got behind the foreign-feeling blue wheel of that blue K-Car. Stomach rolling. Mouth dry. I tried not to think about the worst possible things that could happen. I pulled the door closed, and Jon hopped into the back seat, checking his hair in the rearview mirror. I stole glances at him, glad I had reapplied my lip gloss right after school. I was so anxious; I felt the sweat under my arms flooding that extra deodorant, but I also felt a little warm and buzzy inside, as any girl would sitting two feet away from Jon and getting at least a sliver of his attention. The final time I looked in the rearview, he gave me a small smile and I thought I would burst with happiness.

Mr. Woods not-so-subtly cleared his throat and brought me back to the task at hand. He was all clipboard, all business. He started the "preflight" instruction ritual: Put on the seatbelt. Adjust the mirrors. Find the gas and brake pedals. Find the controls for the headlights and the wipers. Start the car: Put the key in the ignition and turn. "Just start it. Ready?"

Neither of the guys in the car knew I had an embarrassing secret: I had never started a car. Never even came close. In this regard, my father really let me down. He was a true car guy, a gearhead, even. And he had never shown me how to start a car. Maybe it didn't occur to him. Maybe he tried to get me to do it once, and I got too flustered, and he got too impatient. Maybe I was just too dramatic, too emotional. Maybe, and this was more likely, it was because I was a girl. I mean, my brother had been starting cars, and who knows what else, since he was twelve. But here I was, on that cold day, sweating behind the steering wheel of the Chrysler. My shameful secret would be exposed in a matter of seconds. And, to make things so much worse, it would be in front of the cutest of cute boys, in the back seat. He might tell the whole school what an L for loser I was. I felt ashamed.

Mr. Woods handed me the silver car keys, one for the ignition, one for the trunk, on a generic key ring. Attached was a wrinkled white paper circle with the car number in Sharpie. I must have looked panicked, because he said, "Uh, the square one starts the car." I took a deep breath, and with my left hand tightly gripping the steering wheel, I shakily leaned forward, stuck the key into the ignition, and intuitively knew which way to turn it, and I did. I pegged that key to the right, not understanding that I was supposed to let go, until Mr. Woods said, "Ho, ho, that's good, it's running, it's running!" I realized I had been holding my breath and finally exhaled with a shutter. I could only assume Mr. Woods noticed I had no idea what I was doing. I could recite every rule of the road: what color snowplow lights were, the default speed on a residential street, but I didn't know the first thing about this steel mechanical box, and how to make it move. My nerves were firing like 4th of July sparklers, and I hadn't even made it out of the school parking lot. I hadn't moved us anywhere.

After a minute or two of listening to the car engine hum, with the occasional knock thrown in, Mr. Woods said, "Okay, Gilmore, let's take 'er out for a spin." I took yet another deep breath to steady myself. You can do this, I said to myself, you can do this. I was ready, and I went for it. And by that, I mean I really went for it. Before Mr. Woods saw what I was doing, I gripped the steering wheel with my left hand, and put my right hand on the key, in the ignition, ready to start the car. Again. While it was running.

And, because I was feeling much more confident, I gave that key a good crank to the right. And I kept cranking. The most hellacious, snarling, metallic grinding sound started in the ignition and poured into the mouth of the engine.

"Stop, stop, STOP!," yelled Mr. Woods. My hand flew off the key like it had stung me, and l looked in the rearview mirror. Jon was smirking, and trying not to laugh. The fact he didn't guffaw at this situation, at me, was so kind I found him even more endearing if that was possible.

I didn't know what to do, so I just gripped the vinyl steering wheel (at 10 and 2 position) until my hands were red, my knuckles were white, and I stared straight ahead through the windshield. I was dreading what would come next, and I tried to stop it, but it was no use. I started to blush, from pure mortification, from the top of my chest to the top of my head. My blush was not a pretty, subtle pink flush to the cheeks. When I blushed, my body went to war with my emotions. The particular color of red that appeared on my skin was angry, blotchy, and aggressive. I looked like I either had a terrible tanning bed incident, or had been stung repeatedly by a deranged insect, and I never felt more ugly. I was horrified, as my body ordered up flares and kept pushing them out on my skin. I don't think a word had been invented to describe exactly how I felt. I wanted to cry. I wanted to be invisible. I wanted to rewind time fifteen minutes, and I wanted Jon to forget what he saw. I wanted to quit. I wanted to die.

Mr. Woods, to his credit, lit another cigarette, gave me a second to compose myself, and said, "Look, it's no big deal, it happens. Let's just put 'er in gear, D for drive, and get you out on the road." He finished smoking the cigarette (his third, so far, and the car had yet to move) and stubbed it out in the ashtray. I cautiously shifted the car into drive, looked every way possible for traffic in the school parking lot, and slowly drove, or maybe better described, rolled down to the parking lot exit. I gently came to a full stop, turned on my right turn signal, and crept out on the street. I thought, I'm driving! I'm doing it! Mr. Woods' foot continuously hovered over his brake pedal. I think he only stomped it once, when I nearly ran a stop sign, after being distracted by seeing my friend Amanda in the crosswalk in front of me.

After about fifteen minutes of driving, which is to say, fifteen minutes of me carefully steering the blue car from one place to another, "You can go a lot faster, Gilmore – it's a 30 in here," it was time to pull over and give Jon his turn. With pulling over came new own challenges since I had no idea how to transition the car from the street to the curb. I took my best shot at cranking the wheel at a 90-degree angle and rolling nose-first into the curb, which then necessitated me slamming the car into reverse, and backing up on the fairly busy street. That was terrifying – for me, sure, but also for Mr. Woods and Jon. I glanced at their faces each time I gunned the engine, took off for the curb, at various speeds and angles, and then backed up. At this point, neither of them looked particularly encouraging. After four tries, Mr. Woods directed me down the street to the Lutheran church parking lot for the handoff. That was appropriate, as during this inaugural lesson, there was a lot of praying going on, at least by me.

I had wasted more than half my lesson on driving disasters—starting the car, restarting the car while it was running, almost running over Amanda, trying not to drive over the curb. When I got out and took my spot in the backseat, I felt both intensely relieved and humiliated. Just another thing I'm bad at, I thought. By that age, I already had a long catalog of my failures and shortcomings.

Jon got into the driver's seat, clicked his seatbelt, adjusted the mirrors, checked his hair, and started the car like a pro. He reminded me of those guys you see on the highway, driving with their left hand perched on the top of the steering wheel, right arm casually resting on the back of the bench seat. Or with their right arm around their girl, who was scooched next to them. Jon looked so relaxed, so casual, as he drove up and down Plum Street, 7th Street, and Bush Street, at a respectable speed, smoothly stopping at stop signs, and signaling his turns at the right time, not two blocks too soon. I don't think Mr. Woods had to use his brake pedal at all.

Mr. Woods dropped me off at my house at the end of that lesson, and my mother asked how it went. I screeched "FINE!," followed by tears of shame and frustration, stomping, door slamming, and Pink Floyd blasting from my stereo. The following sessions went better, I mean, how could they not, and eventually I was a semi-competent driver.

After I completed the driving lessons with Mr. Woods and got my certificate, I still needed significant practice if I was going to pass my behind-the-wheel test. Someone would have to supervise. My father didn't exactly jump up and volunteer to teach me anything, but after just one ride, it was unanimously decided that my mother was NOT the person for the job. The dramatic gasping, the clutching of the dash, the escalating directions: Turn. TURN. TURN! made for a pretty miserable ride for both of us.

My father's driving lessons were more about practice rather than instruction. That spring when I was almost 16, he perched his tall, bony frame on our cement front steps. From there, he surveyed his kingdom – the front yard, the cement driveway, the mailbox – and watched me drive laps around the racetrack of our street – once gravel, now paved and an imperfect quarter mile circle with eleven houses settled around it – The Circle.

It should be noted that since I only had my learner's permit, I was technically required to have an adult with me in the car at all times. Either my father didn't think about that or didn't care that our sessions were probably illegal.

Tork's parking spot was beside the house, outside my parents' bedroom. At the beginning of each driving "lesson," I opened the heavy driver's door, careful not to hit the yellow wood siding. I started Tork, and slowly backed down the driveway. I eventually arrived at the street, pulled out, and drove and drove around The Circle, first lap – lap – lap around to the right, then lap—lap—lap to the left, switching directions in Bill Schulz's wide driveway. My father insisted I maintain a steady speed of 25 mph. It was clear that I was not cut out for NASCAR.

My father sat and smoked Benson & Hedges cigarettes, pack after pack, gathering the butts, just filters, really, in a little metal ashtray. He had a highball glass with two fingers, or sometimes three, depending on the time of day, of Cutty Sark whiskey, or a white mug of Lipton's tea next to him. Sometimes he brought out the local Republican Eagle newspaper, the Auto Trader, or the Weekly Shopper to give him something to look at while I drove.

During those sessions, as I was driving along, he would look up and make hand gestures toward me. Usually, I could not decode them with the expanse of The Park between us. He could have been signaling the need for tighter turns or warning me not to run over the neighbor kid, for all I knew. Later, I would hear from him how I didn't follow his directions.

Each time my father and I had our practice sessions, I was timid and jumpy, wanting to live up to his high standards, not disappoint him, or worse, get teased. I was so rattled, that I sometimes forgot what he had just told me about parallel parking, or how to turn on the hazard lights. It was probably comical for him to see me frequently slamming on the breaks at 25 mph. As a child, my father learned how to drive a truck out on the ranch in Sheridan County, Nebraska. According to him, he could barely see over the steering wheel and had to sit on a pile of blankets. I believed him.

Based on this, we could never relate to one another's driving experiences, or life experiences in general. He reminded me often that he attended the "school of hard knocks," and he made it clear that he thought my life was one of privilege and comfort. He and my mother had finally clawed up into the ranks of the middle class, but there were still signs that money was tight. My father thought I was dramatic and ungrateful. He had no idea what had happened to me, and what I carried with me. I was terribly unequipped to deal with my trauma, and he was a man of a generation who would not know to ask. We would continue our standoff for many years, him hardboiled in his belief that I was spoiled, and me convinced he should have done something to keep me safe, or at the very least, notice I was unwell. When he and my mother sent me to a male psychiatrist for my eating disorder and I refused to talk, my father made it clear that he thought I was just being stubborn.

I practiced driving for hours and I really thought I got much better and more confident. My father only rode with me once, and said to my mother afterward, "I almost shit my pants!" I had disappointed him once again. That was the end of his ride-alongs. I was eventually allowed to drive my mother the single mile to my grandmother's house, and I drove her downtown, once. Nobody suggested I should take over the Sunday drive-to-Mass responsibilities.

Following the final few practices before I took my behind-the-wheel test, my father's feedback was gruff and non-committal—*that was alright,* or *guess you didn't kill anybody.* By then, we both kind of enjoyed the engagement – being together but at arm's length because that's how we were. I often felt I was orbiting around his universe.

I passed that behind-the-wheel test the first time I took it. When it came time to parallel park, I used the strategy Mr. Woods taught me. During our driving lessons, we realized I had terrible depth perception, due to one eye being nearsighted and the other farsighted. We had developed a plan and practiced it. I reversed, jackknifed into the space at the correct angle, stopped, and politely refused to do the rest of the challenge. If I hit the cones, which was likely, due to nerves, eyesight, or lack of practice, I would automatically fail. The test supervisor nodded, lifted his pen to his clipboard, and automatically docked me points. That was fine with me. At the end of the exam, he handed me my yellow, paper temporary license, I got my photo taken, and I drove myself home in the April sunshine.

The Monaco Grand Prix (As One Does)

My brother and I have, in the soft space of middle age, learned to bond in different ways. We're more than six years apart, and when we were children, we had nothing in common besides shared DNA and living under the same roof, he with his Scooby Doo wallpaper and me with my pink and white Swiss dots. We had to navigate, each in our own way, life with our parents. They could be both generous and kind, cold and punishing. They were the same toward us as they were to each other.

Their rules for my brother and me were unwritten, as far as I could tell. There was always some gray area that allowed them to flex, based on the situation, especially when I was a teenager. I have to admit I was horrible. Maybe not horrible, but difficult. Dramatic. Secretive. Sensitive. Sneaky. But I had reasons for my behavior, based on what had been done to me. So sure, my parents had some basic rules for Tim and me, like don't steal, do well in school, go to Mass on Sunday, and don't talk back. It was that last one that got me in trouble when I was fifteen and sixteen and earned me a couple of hard, open-handed smacks across the face by my father. In his defense, I can understand why he hit me, as a reflex. No parent loves to have FUCK YOU! screamed at them at full volume by their kid.

After he smacked me, and it only happened twice, both

times in the kitchen, I threatened to call the police and report him for child abuse. He told me to go right ahead because he'd be happy to tell them about my antics, my drama, and what he and my mother had to put up with. I would be the one who would get in trouble, not him, he said. They probably wouldn't even believe me, he said. I got as far as the tan wall phone in the kitchen but never picked up the receiver. I turned, stomped to my room, and slammed the door so hard it rattled in the door frame. I cranked up my stereo, probably blasting Judas Priest or AC/DC, and earned a GODDAMMIT, TURN THAT DOWN! from my father, as I flopped on my bed.

 My father hated the door slamming. He hated it so much that when I came home from school one day in the tenth grade, he had removed the door from its hinges, and my room was now completely open to the hallway, affording no privacy. As a young woman who had endured the violations of sexual abuse, that punishment was more horrible than he ever knew. I felt so exposed, so vulnerable, naked. I changed clothes in the bathroom with the door locked. I stopped wearing nightgowns and switched to sweat pants. I felt safer that way. Covered. I can't remember how long the door was gone, probably only a few days or maybe a week. At first, in defiance, I boldly rolled the volume up on my stereo at every opportunity and left my wet towel on the floor and plates in my room (guaranteed irritants to my parents.) But soon, I couldn't stand the feelings I got whenever I saw that empty hole, that opening into my room. My anger melted into fear. I was frustrated with myself – it was just a stupid door – but with the buzzy undercurrent of anxiety, I couldn't sleep, even though I could hear my mother and father snoring in the room next door. With the door gone, there was no longer a barrier between me and what could happen, especially at night. That fear drove me to become a model daughter, at least until I earned back my door privilege, which was what my father called it. I have never forgotten that door incident and how it felt, like another violation, this time of my privacy rather than my body. I never told my friends what happened.

I studied both of my parents, closely, and constantly, and I was never able to figure either of them out. I think they felt the same way about me. My mother never fought her own battles with me, rather, she deployed my father as her personal lieutenant when she was tired of dealing with me. The phrase "Wait 'til your father gets home!" always made my heart pound, but didn't stop me from shrieking back at her. I may have been reckless, but I sure had guts.

Tim and I only spent the required amount of time together growing up. Our family often had dinner together in the evening, especially in the earlier years, when my mother still cooked for us from recipes, and attendance was mandatory. As time went on, my parents' drinking got worse, and by the time I was in junior high, I made dinner for us kids on the nights it was obvious my mother was not coming out of the basement to do it. I craved independence from a very young age, and I knew money was the way to get there. I started babysitting at age 11, got a job as a waitress at 16, and worked at the Red Owl grocery store before I went to college. I wanted nothing more than to get away from my small town and get away from everything that happened there. I felt extremely driven but also excited about my new start.

Tim told me recently that he felt a little abandoned when I left home. I forgot that when I left for college, he was only twelve years old. I had always assumed he enjoyed being the only child, as I did before he was born. But when I stopped to really think about it, he was growing up in that house near the peak worst times of our parents' alcoholism. He had to grow himself up, just like I did, but in a different way. I grew up fast to try to extricate myself from the abuse and to take care of Tim. He had to parent himself, because our parents, deep in their disease, couldn't reliably do so. They were financially generous, sure, and did the best they could, but based on the slurry phone calls from my mother, and the litany of things she was forgetting, the situation was not great. Our grandmother, Eleanor, stepped in as she could, though she was by then in assisted living, and starting to lose her memory. Tim had great friends to support him. As I think back, we had completely different experiences growing up. I was born into the no-money, but less alcohol years, and I was, for the most part, alone. Lonely. Tim grew up, after I left, in the comfortable middle class but had to deal with the turmoil and unpredictability of substance abuse. All that is to say, I feel confused. I feel real regret because I didn't consider how my moving away was going to impact Tim. I have to remember that I was also only 18 years old, barely more than a child myself. I knew that I just had to get out, to save myself, but now I feel an older-sister guilty responsibility for leaving him behind. I don't know how to reconcile that. There is no way to go back and fix it.

But since our parents died, our mother in 2001 and our father in 2004, Tim and I have been orphans together. For twenty years it has been strange because there was just so much stress, noise, and worry when they were alive, and now things are so different. Silent. Tim was only 28 when our mother died, and I wish for him that he could have been around her in the earliest days I remember. The recipe days, the birthday parties, and the special dress days. I wish he could have also sat near our father when he was reading the paper or watching a western on TV, without a drink in his hand, and catch just a little of the warmth he had in those early days when I was little.

Now that it's just us, Tim and I have become closer, even an approximation of friends. Neither of us is particularly demonstrative, so we've had to figure out our path to togetherness. We have the peculiar connection that I'm sure siblings of any age have when they have been orphaned, left behind. We like to spend time together, go places and do things together, and I'm usually the planner. Tim has the veto power. Tim is so even-keeled, that he'll usually go along with most things, unless it's crowds of people, which, ironically, is where we've had some of our best times together. Music festivals. Adventures. Car events.

Tim is like our father in so many ways. Tall. Smart. Mechanical. Droll. And outwardly, unemotional for the most part. Though, as the saying goes, still waters run deep. My brother is every bit as much of a car enthusiast as our father was, maybe more so. He loves all things cars: NASCAR, car shows, Formula One (F1) racing. We take photos of weird cars on the road, like the bizarre Maserati/Blazer mashup vehicle we saw recently, driven by an older man in a red beret. Tim has a seemingly bottomless capacity to remember model numbers, vehicle statistics, and parts, and understand the mysterious inner workings of most things with an engine. I envy him for that ability. The ability to remember, retain. I don't know if he envies me for anything. I've never asked. Throughout my life, my struggle with numbers and memory has left me with one foot rooted in the glory of earned success and the other rooted in the shame of disability and uncertainty.

While our father was alive and for years after he was gone, Tim curated our father's car collection of about a dozen vehicles in a pole shed building we all called Le Garage, that was set along the highway, just outside of my small hometown. The collection was an eclectic grouping, boasting, at various points, a Model T, a 1972 MG convertible, a Tommy Lift truck, a 1974 Ford Galaxie 500, two Corvettes, and a Trans Am convertible, among others. There was also a school bus my father had bought at an auction because it was such a great deal, only a few hundred dollars. He loved running up the bid at local auctions, and then ducking out at the last moment. Except for the times he miscalculated, and ended up with a boat with a bowling ball-sized hole in the hull, boxes full of eggbeaters, rusty tools and musty books, and the bus. That white bus sat rusting outside Le Garage for a decade until my brother was able to sell it for scrap.

In his later years, our father could afford to buy vehicles he liked, and random opportunities for ownership appeared. He was an avid reader of The Auto Trader, and he was a passionate early eBay user and researcher on the bourgeoning internet. Most of the vehicles he purchased had solid, but not fancy, provenance or pedigrees. For example, the Model T belonged to my great uncle Cedric before he died. Then there was the 1962 Corvette. Our father purchased that car from a friend's cousin-in-law in the early 1990s, and it was beautiful. With a sparkly Honduras Maroon paint job and white leather interior, it had precious few miles on it. When our father purchased the Corvette, he wrote off the whole purchase price as a business advertising expense. He was crafty like that. Our father loved that car, and it was proudly driven in the 4th of July and River City Days parades in our small town. It was also shown with pride at local car shows in the park down by the Mississippi River, with the name of my parents' business displayed on the dashboard placard. It made more than one appearance at the massive Back to the Fifties car show at the Minnesota State Fairgrounds, alongside

10,000 other cars. I have a lot of photos of Tim sitting by the car in a lawn chair, squinting into the summer sun, a beer in his hand, sometimes with friends, sometimes alone.

    I have no photos of me sitting with the 1962 Corvette at a car show, squinting into the sun. Or with any of the other cars in my father's collection. For many years I've wondered why. If I was excluded, and why? Or if I simply took myself out of the equation, and why? I think it was chicken and egg, cause and effect. A Mobius loop. My father had not shown interest in teaching me about cars, so I had not shown him interest in learning about cars. This paradoxical cycle had served to nudge me outside the inner circle of car people in my family. I leaned in as a longing and curious bystander, but not someone immersed in the intricacies of their car culture. I didn't read the car magazines that were piled on my parents' coffee table. I didn't know the words or speak the language. I could barely check the oil in my car. I was not one of them. And it did not feel good. I was always low-key jealous of my brother and the connection he had with our father. Between them, if there was nothing else, if they avoided talking about everything else, there were always cars and car things to discuss.

    The feeling of being an outsider to the family car culture could have very well started with the fact that in my family, as I suppose with all car families, cars and math went hand in hand. Back-of-the-envelope penciled calculations, socket sets, wrenches, bottles, and cans of oil, festooned with numbers. As a person with an undiagnosed learning disability, dyscalculia, no one knew my brain could not process numbers, do math, or identify those labels at a normal speed. As far back as when I was five or six, during the sweetest time and attention I craved with my father, in the garage on a Saturday or Sunday afternoon, I struggled with handing him the right size socket or wrench, when he asked me to firmly drop it in his palm, like a surgical instrument in the operating theater, to repair or bring life to an automobile or lawnmower or boat engine. I never seemed to get it right the first time, and I tried his patience. Eventually, I was not invited to "car time" with him. He could do it himself. Eventually, when my brother was old enough, he took over as the helper.

The struggle with numbers stayed with me, like a fever that never broke. My father and I spent countless nights at the wooden kitchen table, him trying to explain how to carry numbers in multiplication, over and over, showing on scratch paper how simple long division was, if I "just paid more attention." We sat across from one another for hours, getting more frustrated, more angry, and convinced the other was not listening at all. Inevitably, my father would push his chair back with a sigh, saying "That's enough for one night," and head for the basement, glasses of Scotch, and the solace of television.

I would try to puzzle out worksheet after worksheet, scrubbing holes into the paper with the pencil eraser. Eventually, alone I would dissolve into messy tears of exasperation, stomp into my bedroom and slam the door. My inability to conquer the worksheets, show my work, and get the right answers was further reinforced at school, as a deep character flaw. My fifth-grade Catholic school teacher, Miss Campbell, the former nun, after depositing yet another completed worksheet covered in red ink on my desk, decided to make an example of me. I was her cautionary tale. Her worst-case scenario. She announced to the class that I "shouldn't plan on amounting to anything," with my laziness, and my lack of attention to detail. It would do no good to protest. I felt so much shame.

In my sophomore year of high school, I was relegated to "dummy math" with the athletes and stoners. The wrestling coach was the teacher, and he quickly recognized my efforts to learn. The bar was pretty low in that class. Several times a week, he sat patiently with me after school, as I tried to decode the basic tenants of geometry. I got a C+. It was a triumph. In college, I repeated Math 100. The second time through, the professor told me I deserved a C just for showing up. I graduated with a BA in liberal studies, rather than the marketing degree I had planned. It didn't matter. I walked away with my diploma, elated, and with the knowledge I would never, ever pick up another math book.

It wasn't until I was 40 that I was formally diagnosed with dyscalculia, and it was an immense relief. I have a disability. I wasn't just bad at math. I wasn't stupid. My brain doesn't have the gears in the machinery to properly digest and decode numbers and align them the way other people see them. I could live with that, but I also kept it a secret. From family, friends, coworkers, and bosses. In my mind, dyscalculia was still a serious flaw, character or not. My father never knew about my disability. I could not bring back those missed hours of connection in the garage, those opportunities. It was too late to resolve decades of longing. He was already gone.

In our soft middle age, my interest in bonding over car things, cars, and car culture with my brother became stronger. For his 40th birthday, I gifted Tim 40 laps of driving the Talladega Speedway race track in a NASCAR, and he had a blast. I was the photographer. For his 50th birthday, I wanted to do something even bigger. He had mentioned over the years how cool the F1 Monaco Grand Prix was. Those confident, arrogant Formula One drivers, performing in an environment that dripped history and money and privilege. I booked our trip and made a 16-page PowerPoint agenda for us. The trip was a big deal for both of us, and I wanted everything to go smoothly.

I had arranged a car to pick us up at the airport in Nice, and we were delighted that the car was a white Porsche sedan. We felt, if not like royalty, like people with money, real money. We giggled in the back seat. We stayed in a lovely hotel on the waterfront in Nice, and sipped Aperol spritzes and beers at the outdoor cafes. Every time we did something bougie like that, we would say, "as one does," and then laugh and laugh. The train to Monaco was quiet in the morning and packed on the way back.

We explored Monaco by foot, both because the principality is very compact, and because traffic was slug-like during race weekend. In front of one of the most luxurious hotels in town, the Hotel Hermitage Monte-Carlo, we spied what appeared to be a very exclusive, extraordinary car show. The cars were spectacular: Rolls Royce, Maybach, Lamborghini, Bugatti, McLaren, one after the other. After a while, we realized it wasn't an intentional car show – these vehicles belonged to guests of the hotel. It was great entertainment, checking out those millions and millions of dollars-worth of automobiles. I'm sure Tim got tired of my rapid-fire and repetitive, "What's that?" every time we saw something new, and "How much is that?" once the vehicle was identified. He is a patient man.

During the Monaco Grand Prix qualifying event, Tim and I sat in the stands and with earplugs in place, cheered on our favorites, at least I did, as the cars came zzzzzZZZZZZzzzzzmmm around the track like buzzsaws. Tim absorbed and enjoyed. I had surreptitiously been studying up on the top drivers for Mercedes (yay, Louis Hamilton!), Ferrari, Red Bull, and the rest, so I could at least cheer appropriately, or try my best. It was late May, and quite unseasonably hot and steamy for qualifying, and our backs were soaked in salty sweat. The lines for water were long. We breathed in the gassy fumes from the scorching asphalt tarmac, and the reek of roasting black tires. It was glorious.

Race day started overcast, and then it rained in dense,

white, punishing downpours. Water gushed off the ridged metal benches and poured into our shoes. Our disposable rain ponchos barely kept up. The race was suspended more than once, and from the metal bleachers, we saw celebrities across the track from us, sipping cocktails and chatting in the paddocks. I can confirm that Tom Cruise is not tall. At long last, the clouds tightened up, and the race was on. The air crackled with humidity and anticipation, and we craned our necks to see the F1 cars chasing the pace car. I grinned as I sat wedged in amongst the thousands of hot, cheering, drenched car people that day in Monaco. I realized, at that moment, that I was a car person too.

AS THE CROW FLIES

The Garage

In the early 1970s, our young neighborhood in Fremont California was changing. Original owners were starting to move out, move up, to larger homes. The perfect landscaping, pristine ivory stucco, and clean cement driveways started showing signs of wear and neglect. Renters were coming in.

In those days, kids as young as six, like I was, roamed freely, completely unsupervised, in the neighborhood. My mother worked five days a week, my father six. During their brief time off, they had stuff to do. Laundry to wash, groceries to get, lawn to mow, car to wash, oil to change. As an only child, I was often bored. After checking out our trees in the backyard (lemon, lime, plum) for any ripe fruit, I would peek through the gaps in our redwood fence to see what the neighbors were doing. I was a nosy little kid. Then I would go exploring. I would turn left out of our driveway, and walk four or five blocks until I got to the large house on the corner with the two giant dogs. Those monsters were fenced in the side yard, and I tried, mostly unsuccessfully, to sneak by them. They were like the troll under the bridge in the fairy tales, but scarier. I was terrified of large dogs since a daycare lady I had when I was four years old thought it was funny to let her German shepherds race up to me and knock me over every day when we went in the backyard to swim in her above-ground pool. Those dogs, three or four of them, would bark, never in unison, and jump all over me, as I cowered as best I could on the ground, crying hysterically. I think I remember her laughing.

During my adventures around the neighborhood, when those neighborhood dogs caught sight of me, their growls started as a baritone rumble deep in their chests, and built to a thunderous explosion of sound from their mouths. They were black and brown and muscular and would leap, slobbering, jagged teeth on full display, wild-eyed, their weight straining the chain link fence. They couldn't get at me through the fence, but I didn't understand that. I would turn and sprint toward home, small feet pounding the sidewalk. On the way home, I often encountered small neighborhood gangs of siblings, who either ignored me or chased me down the sidewalk to pull my blonde pigtails, call me names, or shake me down for the pennies and nickels I sometimes had in my pocket. Like my father, I enjoyed the sound the jangling coins made when I walked. I always traveled solo, as I had no siblings, and few friends in the neighborhood. Few friends, period.

Then that year, as a complete surprise, my parents had announced I would have a new brother or sister. I was giddy. I longed for a sister and tacked that wish onto my prayers every night at bedtime. Pleasebringmeababysister. Amen.

My brother was born several months later. I was crushed. A brother. My parents let me name him Timmy. Maybe that name was their idea, and they just let me think it was mine. I got to bring him to show and tell in my first-grade class so that removed some of the sting.

One late spring day, a moving truck rolled up in front of the chocolate brown house kitty-corner from us. A bunch of guys, along with an older man, and all their boxes, belongings, and furniture, moved in. I didn't see any kids my age, which was very disappointing. Having new neighbors was exciting, nonetheless. The guys were probably in their late teens and early twenties. To my six-year-old self, they were all grown-ups. And I was very curious.

As soon as my parents would let me, I marched over to the brown house and introduced myself to the guys, telling them all about the neighborhood, like a mini–Welcome Wagon lady. All I was missing was a pink suit and pearls. I imagine my cheerful and comprehensive welcome to the neighborhood was pretty amusing to them. I informed them where the gas station was, and how to find my elementary school, and cautioned them about the giant dogs down the street.

Once they settled in, those boys blasted Jethro Tull, Deep Purple, and Alice Cooper, at all hours, from big brown speakers they hung on the wall in the space I came to call The Garage. Sometimes the neighbors complained about the noise. I know my dad called the cops on them more than once. I, on the other hand, accepted the noise as my entrance fee into the magical world of The Garage. The music scared me a little, though I always tried to look brave, despite the thump-thump-thump of the bass guitar pounding my eardrums. It was always a shock walking up their driveway after very little transition time from my side of the street, and the bland and steady diet of Andy Williams, The Kingston Trio, Frank Sinatra, and the Elvis Presley love songs my parents played on repeat on our record player.

My dad disparagingly called the guys "greasers," as they were always in The Garage or on their driveway, especially on the weekends, working on something with an engine, wearing ripped t-shirts and jeans, smearing their oily hands on ratty, red rags or their skinny thighs. My dad's condemnation said a lot since he worked in a muffler shop, but he still managed to have clean fingernails. My father was fastidious about his hands. There was always a can of Boraxo powdered soap and a nail brush on the laundry tub, and that was his first stop when he came home from work. He valued cleanliness and organization, and always took good care of the things he had. He said that just because a person didn't have money, they didn't have to look low-class and dirty.

Whenever the double garage door was lifted open at the brown house, you could see The Garage was far different than ours. My dad swept the concrete floor in our garage with a special push broom. Everything was in its place: tools, mower, potting soil, Christmas decorations. Unlike our garage, The Garage was an explosion of tools, red rags, orange air filter boxes, rubber hoses, and belts, weird-looking metal things, beer bottles, and tires. There was always at least one chopper motorcycle and a car, hood propped up, undergoing some type of repair, and mysterious parts and pieces piled on the floor. The Garage smelled like motor oil, gasoline, and the ripe odors of sweaty men and beer. Sometimes it smelled like pizza. There was often an empty pizza box or two on the workbench. There were metal ramps and jacks to elevate cars just enough that the guys could wheel the creepers underneath. I was worried a car could fall on one of them, because once at my father's muffler shop, the hydraulic jack failed and the vehicle he was working on came down on top of him. He was trapped in the crawl space underneath until a customer eventually came in, sometime later. He was lucky he didn't die.

    In The Garage, there were glass jars of every size, with nails, screws, and bolts, haphazardly lined up on the battered and scarred wooden workbench that ran the full length of the right-side wall. Some were baby food jars. I wondered how they got so many because there were no babies on their side of the street. There were Butternut coffee cans, but I was too short to see what was inside them. Above the workbench, was a massive brown chipped pegboard that was covered with rows and rows of uniform little holes, a good many filled with dull gray metal holders or hooks that fit perfectly in the holes. Each of the holders was important because they held the Craftsman screwdrivers, worn pliers, both regular and needle-nose, wrenches, rachet drivers, and two ball peen hammers, along with other tools, just like in our garage. But in our garage, there was a blue and white debossed label, fresh out of the label maker for each tool, so it would be returned to the right place after using it. In The Garage, sometimes one of the guys would lift me so I could plug in one of the pegboard hooks or grab a tool. I was so thrilled, I'd just grin, showing my missing front teeth. My greatest hope was that one day, the boys would let me use those tools, and show me how to fix a car. I just knew I could do it. I couldn't wait to show my father. He would be so proud.

Even though this was a man's place, filled with men, their swearing and shouts and laughter, the smell of sweaty armpits, the blare of music from the speakers, and the constant clanking of tools hitting metal, I never felt afraid. Even though I had been surviving sexual abuse for more than a year whenever my grandfather visited, and I should have had the sense to start fearing all men, I felt safe in The Garage. Those boys created my refuge.

I never saw a mom at that house. Sometimes long-haired girls were hanging around The Garage, sitting in lawn chairs, smoking, and wearing crochet tops and bell-bottom jeans. They were nice to me. I thought they were pretty. Sometimes they would braid my hair, and sometimes they would sing along to the music. We were interrupted frequently by the guys. They yelled for the girls to bring them beers or grab their smokes. The girls did not work on the vehicles and ignored my questions about tires and engines.

The cement driveway in front of The Garage was always occupied by one or more cars, in various stages of disrepair, some with dubious chances of being resurrected. The guys would sometimes work outside on the driveway, but usually, they would just roll a car into The Garage. Before they moved a car inside, they always yelled at me to get on the grass, out of the way, even though I wanted to help push the cars. There were blobby oil spots scattered everywhere on the driveway, suspicious-looking red and green stains, too. The red ones made me feel a little scared like birds had maybe died there.

Even as a six-year-old, I could see the relationship between my parents and the guys in the brown house was tense. My father would go ballistic when nails and screws would roll (or be flung) down the driveway of the brown house and end up in the gutter and on the street. Twice, my mother got a flat tire (screw in the tread) on our tan Volkswagen Squareback. Each time, my father went marching across the street in a rage. My dad was tall and rangy, six-three and tough. I got the feeling when he went over to yell at the guys, even though he was furious, he may have been a little apprehensive. In California at that time, The Hell's Angels were on the rise. The black leather jackets the guys wore had a red and white coat of arms on the back. They wore those jackets when they rode their motorcycles, even when it was hot, and hung them on hooks in The Garage.

I think those jackets had something to do with the Hell's Angels, but I can't prove it. I found out later that my dad had started taking a pistol with him to the muffler shop at that time, which I know for a fact had something to do with the Hell's Angels. I heard my parents talking about it. My father was well-known as "the guy" in the Bay Area for custom exhaust and mufflers, for cars and motorcycles. I remember him saying at the dinner table that his boss, Jerry, initially encouraged him to get the extra business the "Angels" would bring to the shop, and my father resisted. He said that if you did work for one, you were signing up to do work for all of them. At some point, he finally acquiesced. My father was a perfectionist, did great work, and there was a strong sense of mutual respect between the Angels and my father. The last thing my father wanted was to have a business dispute with the Hell's Angels. The gun was never out of his reach.

Once, when I was visiting The Garage, one of the guys gave me a little ride on the back of a newly repaired chopper. Of course, there weren't any helmets, certainly not in a size for my small head. We drove down the middle of our street, as slowly as possible, engine vibrating, pipes rumbling, me clutching the driver's sides for dear life, and smiling so hard my face hurt. I felt like I belonged. I felt a taste of freedom. Unfortunately, my mother caught a glimpse of my joyride and told my father. That caused another pissed-off stomp across the street. For years, whenever I remembered that day on the motorcycle I felt warm and happy. I felt something like love.

The absolute best part about going across the street, though, was the soda machine. There was a real Coke machine in The Garage, that held glass bottles of beer and soda. The machine was always plugged in and buzzing. It was an old-fashioned model, with a red body and a heavy lid you lifted when you wanted to get a bottle. This machine didn't take money, as the guys had disabled that function. So you just opened the lid and reached in, grabbed a bottle by the neck, and it came loose with a satisfying metallic clunk. The lid closed with a whomp. I was just a little too short to choose my bottle without help, and there was more than one occasion where I nearly fell inside the machine, head first, while trying. There was a red metal bottle opener on the side of the machine to pop off the cap, which sometimes flew through the air and landed with a bouncing, rolling clink. It was my special job to find all the bottle caps in The Garage and put them in the big ashtray on the metal stand. This job was likely created to keep me out of the way and stop me from asking a million questions. In that magical Coke machine, there was a lot less soda than beer. But almost always, there were a couple of bottles of Coke, and sometimes an Orange Crush, grape soda, or root beer. There were times, however, I showed up and there was nothing for me in the machine. I tried to hide my disappointment. I was pretty sulky, despite my perky blonde pigtails. I turned around and flounced back across the street in protest.

When the soda machine issues were too much to bear, I went home and complained loudly to my parents. I whined about the unfairness of the whole situation. My father would thunder, "What the hell were you doing over there in the first place?" I think he responded that way because he was scared.

That fall, I was six and my first-grade class was visited by two uniformed policemen. They lectured us on the dangers of drugs. I added dope and uppers and downers and bennies to my vocabulary. This was far before D.A.R.E.. There were no color commercials in the early 1970s with eggs frying in a pan, supposedly showing my brain on drugs. Nancy Reagan was busy being First Lady of California, years before she became First Lady of the White House. My parents read the pamphlet the teacher sent home for their signature, and my father exploded. He was shocked and enraged they were teaching first graders, HIS first grader, about drugs. My mother was also upset. I could tell by the way she smoked her cigarette, drawing the smoke in, and releasing it in small, quick, repetitive puffs. I had learned to keep my distance when I saw her smoking like that.

I thought it was somehow my fault my parents were so upset. That I caused this gash in our family fabric. I tried to fix it. For several nights, I stood outside my parents' closed bedroom door in my flowered nightgown. Light slid under the door and melted into the hallway carpet. I could hear my parents speaking in low tones, urgently. For weeks, I was determined to be a model kid. I tried to brush my teeth and say my prayers every night, without reminders.

A year later, my parents announced we were moving to Minnesota, where my Grandma and Grandpa with a basement lived. I had two sets of grandparents with last names starting with G, but only one set of grandparents with a basement, so that's how we differentiated them. I would come to differentiate my grandfathers differently. I was excited to play in the snow in Minnesota. The move was fine by me.

 In the time between the announcement and actually leaving, my parents stated over and over to whomever they were talking to, we were moving to a far better and safer place to raise kids. A lower cost of living. Better values. Closer to family. An ideal place. I'm not sure who they were trying to convince, other people or themselves.

 Our little house sold in a matter of days, and plans were put in place for our reverse migration: back to the Midwest. We couldn't afford a moving company, but my parents hired professional packers. They showed up, organized, and filled the back of the big U-Haul truck so tightly there was not even room for a deck of cards. My father, with his engineering-type sensibilities, was impressed. He purchased a huge, rectangular Master padlock for the back of the truck. He pulled the truck doors together, threaded the lock, clanked the padlock closed, and tested it with a few aggressive tugs. In the morning, he would use the bulbous trailer hitch on the back of the U-Haul to hook up the sturdy tan VW Squareback. The car was crammed full of boxes and bedding, and ready for the long slog to Minnesota.

 That last night, my parents, my toddler brother and I slept

on the floor of our empty house. At dawn, we packed up the last of our things and walked through the house. My father took a few pictures as I said goodbye to the green shag carpeting, the fireplace, the plum tree in the backyard. The four of us made our way down the driveway together. I looked longingly at the brown house and gave it a half-hearted wave. I never got to say goodbye to the boys, to the Coke machine, to The Garage. The new owners of our house were standing at the curb in front of our house, their huge moving truck parked on the street, engine running. I felt leaving combined with an intense sense of loss. It was the first time I felt grief associated with a place. We had left before, plenty of times but I always knew we were coming back. I knew where home was. It was a little stucco house with a brown roof. This time was different, and I understood it was permanent. Closure was impossible. I hoped the boys would not forget me. I have moved many, many times since that summer morning, and only a few other times have I felt what I would learn to call anguish.

My father had carefully planned and documented our exodus eastward. Our route was marked, in pencil, on the pages of the Rand McNally road atlas that never left the bench seat of the U-Haul. State by state, highway by highway, we were heading to the Midwest Promised Land of good grandparents, hotdish, flat vowels, polka music, and cornfields, where first-graders were not talking about uppers and bennies.

My father commanded all things navigation, while my

mother made sure the U-Haul was outfitted each morning with a thermos of gas station coffee, Kleenex, an extra pack of cigarettes, and a few snacks. I rode with my father intermittently, and those miles, perched on the bench seat with him were glorious. I got to push all the radio station buttons, open the snacks, and observe, over and over, my father's smoking ritual. First, he patted his chest pocket, then grabbed the gold pack of Benson & Hedges cigarettes. I heard the crinkling of cellophane under his large palm and saw paper, then foil, then the perfectly formed white tubes lined up inside. My father jostled the pack until a single white cigarette peeked out. He withdrew it with his front teeth. He reached in his pants pocket for his worn metal Zippo lighter. I heard the familiar metallic clink as he flipped it open, a tiny grinding sound as he lit the flame, then the clunk as he closed it, and returned it to his pocket. He inhaled deeply, then exhaled through his nose. I thought that was very sophisticated. Sometimes I could convince him to blow smoke rings, and I clapped. My father would sometimes open the truck window a few inches so the smoke could slither outside. He and I played the car version of the "I Spy" game. I'd guess the make of cars as they passed us on the highway. I was often wrong, unintentionally or on purpose, so he'd tell me facts and features about each one. I was quicker than he was in playing "slug bug," when a Volkswagen Beetle flew by, and I would pop him in the arm and dissolve into giggles.

    My mother, however, lobbied for me to ride with her

to keep an eye on my brother and give her someone to talk to. It caused some friction because riding with her was not fun. She drove the blue and white, flat-nosed Volkswagen bus that my parents purchased after my brother was born. She radiated anxiety and resentment like a teapot that was ready to whistle. When I asked questions, including the ubiquitous how much further? and if our motel would have a pool, and if we were stopping for snacks soon, she responded with a few short, clipped words, usually followed by a directive to just stop asking! We kept in contact with my father via our brand-new set of walkie-talkies. I loved pressing the talk button, sharing inane observations from the road, asking my father the same questions as my mother, and ending every conversation with "over and out!"

On the rare occasions that we were on straight, flat interstates, the weather was good, my brother was sleeping, and there was a song on the radio she liked, my mother would sing along in her gorgeous, clear soprano. For those few minutes, she looked happy as she bopped her head and freed the notes stored somewhere in her body. She looked young. She looked pretty. She looked carefree.

The VW bus had been carefully configured for this trip with a small playpen set up behind the driver's seat for my brother, and a cache of diapers and baby food next to it on the floor. A dark green metal Coleman cooler filled with sandwiches and drinks, cooled by bags of ice we picked up when we filled up with gas every morning, guarded the sliding door. The bus smelled like Pampers, apple juice, cigarette smoke, and loneliness.

The U-Haul towed our brown VW Squareback, and overheated several times in the Colorado Rockies, and my father pulled to the side of the road and eased into rest areas to let the engine temperature cool. We lost valuable hours of daylight as we waited at worn picnic tables and ran around on stubby grass. Sometimes my father held a towel over the radiator cap and swore loudly when he turned the cap and steam escaped like opening a portal into hell. I always wanted to "help" and more than once he shoved me out of the way, so I would not get scalded. In case he needed to top off the radiator, he kept a plastic jug of distilled water in the cab of the U-Haul. It took us five long days to drive more than two thousand miles on that trip. We stayed at budget motels, with the U-Haul and the bus parked in front of our door. I saw my father pull the curtains on the window aside multiple times a night to ensure the truck was unbothered.

We made it to Minnesota with ourselves, the vehicles, and our belongings intact, though my parents' patience had worn thin, and there was a thick layer of irritation between them. My brother was cranky and ready to be sprung from his playpen, and he wobbled and stomped around our new yard in the stiff-legged, flat-footed way of new toddlers. I was overwhelmed by all the new things: house, yard, humidity. We were warmly welcomed on that steamy August day. Neighbors and relatives arrived with hotdishes, sandwiches, and cakes, to celebrate the homecoming of the prodigal daughter and her family.

Our new house was chocolate brown, much like the kitty-corner house in Fremont. That was comforting and felt familiar. The street in front of the house was swathed in coarse tan gravel. As they passed, a small cloud of beige dust lifted and shadowed behind cars and trucks. We had a screened-in porch and a basement of our own. In the following days, the Realtor pulled the SOLD sign out of our front lawn and left a post-sized hole in the grass. We learned about things like potlucks, swimming lessons at the YMCA, and the times of Sunday Mass. I discovered there were mean kids, bullies, and big dogs everywhere. I discovered that the sexual abuse followed me to the Midwest like a stain I couldn't wash off: when my grandfather visited; during sleepovers at the house of my parents' insurance agent; and rides home after babysitting from handsy fathers. Walking home in the dark was terrifying, but at least I knew I could run, even in snow boots or flip-flops. Every branch shifting in the wind, every carried voice or car engine in the distance pushed me to walk faster. Those early years in the Midwest were when I became an expert in worst-case scenarios. An escape artist. I told no one what was happening to me. Thinking back on it, I became brave in, and because of, my isolation.

In the Midwest, there was no place to go, like The Garage. Eventually, I discovered the public library, which became my surrogate refuge. The librarians stood in for the boys, though they were reserved and never laughed. The beanbag chairs at the end of the rows of books in the youth section became my safe place when my fear and anxiety became too much to bear. When the gnawing of my secrets began eating me from the inside out.

Our family slowly adjusted to the smallness of our new town. To the slower pace, the passive-aggressiveness, and the Midwestern work ethic. My mother frequently commented how good it was to be home, to be raising a family in this safe place. I struggled to understand what she meant. The memories I was building were of confusion, of violation, shrouded in loneliness. I longed for The Garage, for my elementary school that served tacos and tamales, not mashed potatoes and gravy on white bread, and for the retired next-door neighbors who watched out for me. Tony and Delores next door let me come over whenever I wanted. They must have sensed my neediness. My loneliness. They were kind. But in this new life, I was constantly on high alert, as if those giant dogs were around every corner. There was newness, and uncertainty. Bullies and predators. And so many secrets to hide.

Why Is Tom In The Trunk?

I've known Marni since we were, happily or not, married to our first husbands. Between us, we've raised six kids and stepkids, and we've been through divorces, deaths, and more houses than I can count on one hand. I remarried, and Marni, for many reasons, has not. But for years, Marni lived with her long-term partner, Tom, a former prosecutor turned lawyer, turned Simpson's memorabilia collector, turned part-time salesman at Total Wine. Tom was smart, witty and sarcastic, and his searing intellect far outlasted his body. As he got into his 50s, Tom grew more and more portly, with the belly of a man who enjoyed good wine and fast food. He began to suffer the debilitating pain of the former athlete who skidded into middle age, complaining more and exercising less. It was an ongoing source of friction in the relationship.

Marni was always active, and she and I walked the Breast Cancer 3-Day together. "It's fun," she said. "San Diego in November will be lovely," she said. It was 60 miles of sucky, exhausting, sweaty, and hellish walking. While thinking about us staggering the 2-1/2-mile slog up to Torey Pines, what sticks in my mind is the expert-level and creative profanity we deployed. I think we may have created a new subgenre called hate limericks.

The swearing sort of made it bearable. Marni's version of profanity has its own glorious lexicon. And, it's not just about exchanging heck for hell, or dang for damn, which is the

Midwestern way.

When frustrated or mad, she'll let loose with a cockadoodie! Or, flippin' motherfucker! Or, god-dammit-I'm-going-to hell! That one usually pops out when we have been talking some serious shit about someone, or saying things about religion that our mothers would definitely not have approved of. But with Marni, I'm never sure what she's going to say and that's part of the fun.

Last October, Marni and I were chatting at the salon where she works as a nail tech, and she was doing my nails. Because we live in Minnesota, the topic turned to the weather. This particular type of weather conversation is as predictable in Minnesota as someone saying, *ope! let me just sneak past ya here*, when you're at the grocery store. I said that even though we had gotten our first snow of the season, I had not yet put my snow brush and winter survival kit in the trunk of my car. My father's voice echoed in the back of my head, with his strict instructions: Never leave home without a blanket, a snow scraper, and $20 in your wallet for emergencies. He did give me this advice in the 1980s when I could have filled my gas tank for $10, and $20 bought enough cheap beer to fuel a pretty solid party. But here it was, mid-October and I was snowbrush-free. Marni said, "Oh shit, I need to do that, too."

The conversation turned to talking about all the things we stuffed in our car trunks over the years, mostly for our kids. In Marni's case, cheerleading gear, in mine, softball, baseball, and football equipment. All of it exuded the unmistakable aroma of teenage hormones, sweaty armpits, and dried grass. Marni and I laughed about the packets of fruit snacks and smashed granola bars we found months and years later, rock-hard artifacts of post-practice demands.

Then Marni giggled and said the week before, her oldest daughter had been visiting from Washington, DC. They were getting ready to go back to the airport, and her daughter opened the trunk of Marni's car to throw in her suitcase. She peered inside at the last moment. "Mooooommmmmmm! Tom's still in here!" Marni said, "Oh, I know he is," with a smile.

Three years prior, Tom had died unexpectedly of a massive heart attack. Marni had come home from work, and found Tom in the darkened house, his phone on the floor, skittered just far enough away from him to be useless. There was shiva and cremation, and the sandy ashes were divided between Tom's family and Marni. The family spread their portion of the ashes after about a year, next to a creek that Tom loved. Now, two more years had gone by, and the box containing Tom, or some of Tom, was still in the trunk of Marni's car, riding around until she could decide when and where she would spread his ashes. It was a huge decision. She had several contenders, including the Burger King drive-thru and the Simpson's Ride at Universal Studios. But the right place and time had not yet presented itself, and Tom stayed in the trunk of Marni's little white Honda, sliding dramatically from one side to the other, whenever she took a sharp corner. "Sorry, buddy!" I pictured her calling out when she heard the shhhhhh, and whomp of the box, as it slid and smacked into the side of the trunk.

Marni shared that she was fine with the fact that 50% of Tom had not yet gone to his eternal rest, or been dumped into the breeze in a meaningful spot. "In fact," she said, "it's really working out great for me." When he was alive, Tom had the uncanny ability to find a good parking spot or even a great spot, no matter where he went. He called it good parking karma. He was the parking ninja, the parking spot whisperer. Marni said while Tom had been hanging out in the trunk of her car, she had AMAZING luck finding great parking places. Even downtown! So, Marni was really in no particular hurry to give all that up. She was matter-of-fact while she was telling me all this while filing my nails, and it took me a beat to realize that she was serious. I must have had a weird, slack-jaw, what-the-hell-Marni look on my face. Then I started to laugh and she joined in. And by a laugh, I mean the kind of laughing that, since we were predisposed to laugh-crying and/or snorting, we were doing both. It was the kind of cleansing laughter that pokes at the muscles in your chest and belly and gives a hard reset, like unplugging the computer. The laughing died down into some sniffing and chuckling, as Marni finished applying pink lacquer to my nails.

As I was leaving the salon, I saw Marni's little white car at the edge of the parking lot, and I smirked. I put my car in reverse and looped around the lot until I was behind the trunk of her car. I paused, waved at Tom, yelled, "Hey buddy! Nice to see you!," and gave the horn a little beep, before I pulled out onto the frontage road, and headed for home.

    I laughed, but I also reflected on all the people I had let go over the years and how many I had told goodbye, or wish I had been able to. Each one of them, in their own way, had enriched my life and shaped me, even if it was through violence, neglect, or pain. I was learning to accept those experiences with gratitude. It was incredibly hard. But I was getting there.

Dancing With The Gravedigger

My father died the night of my 20th class reunion, on a thickly humid and mosquito-filled Minnesota summer Saturday night. During his later years, especially after Samson was born, he had softened and became a little more expressive. After my mother died, he sought my time and attention; he was lonely. But his phone calls, chain emails, and voice messages often went unanswered. I continue to feel sad about that. The guilt still nudges me at times, like an old sliver in my heel. With Sarah and her vast needs, and Samson, and work and a marriage that was inelegantly dissolving, I had little time or energy left to give my father. His COPD was advancing, and he knew his time on this earth was dwindling. He was generous with money and gifts, especially for Samson. He tried his best to be supportive of Sarah's challenges and mine. During one of the last full conversations I had with my father, I told him I was getting divorced. He was not surprised, and he spewed out some colorful language about Chris, which was deeply offensive but also very funny. He said he never understood why we got married in the first place. My father was a smart, sarcastic man, generous, especially in later years.

My relationship with my father was complicated and confusing my whole life. I loved him, and when I was little, I adored him, and I wanted to be just like him. So much so that when I was very young, maybe four, I decided I was going to use his shaving cream and razor and shave just like he did every morning. I thought he would be proud of me. Except the razor was sharp, too sharp, and I ended up slicing a two-inch gash in my lower lip and bleeding all over the bathroom. My uncle found me, and when my father learned what happened, he was not proud at all. I just wanted him to like me and enjoy spending time with me. I was a very precocious little girl, an early reader, and an only child until I was nearly seven, and I was always looking for attention. I accepted what he was able to give me, but I was always wanted, needed more. Those small bits of his time just whet my appetite. I was starving, and he didn't seem to notice. That may be a cause of my neediness, my determined search for love and acceptance later in life. As I got older, my perspective evolved, and I just wanted to like my father more. I wanted him to be different, more like the fathers you see on TV, I guess. More like the fathers some of my friends had. Kinder. Less critical. More understanding. More interested in me. Every time he missed one of my play performances, band concerts, or science fairs, I felt wounded but pretended I did not. He often went to the Elk's Lodge for stag night to drink and play cards instead. I do not doubt that he loved me very much. I just wish that we both had been more emotionally available and that we had been closer.

    His death that July night was unexpected, yet not a complete surprise. He had been sick, but it was shocking how he had gone from eating ice cream and chatting with his grandson, to passing away a day later. He had been battling pneumonia, which he got several times a year due to his end-stage COPD. The day he died, he started coughing during his lunch, and aspirated chocolate pudding. It would have been funny, a punchline in a joke, but he was lying in his hospital bed, zoned out on morphine, barely blinking, until he quietly took his last breath. Tim and I were there when he died, each keeping our own type of vigil. I at my father's bedside, reading *The Devil Wears Prada*. Tim in the visiting area down the hall, flipping through a magazine. Both of us hated that nursing home/rehab facility. Both of us hated that we had to be there. Our father told us many times over the years that he didn't want to "die in a goddamn nursing home." And yet. There we were.

On Monday, Tim and I had an appointment at the small-town funeral home our family had used for generations. This funeral home, all dusty red velvet curtains, paisley carpet, and that weird smell, was where Tim and I would make all the arrangements for our father. He was not a churchgoer, and he was a humble man who didn't want a fuss. At our appointed time, we were ushered into the conference room with its big wooden table, strategically placed tissue boxes, and a stand displaying pamphlets with lilies and clouds on the covers. The three of us sat, my brother and I on one side and the funeral director named Todd, across from us. He wore a dark suit with a white shirt and could have easily been mistaken for a door-to-door missionary, there to share the Good News.

The first order of business was to figure out how Todd should refer to our father. His name was Michael, but only our mother had called him that. To everyone else, he was just Mike. We thought he would prefer it.

From his side of the conference table, Todd spoke softly, in a low register, with what I can only imagine was intended to be a soothing and comforting tone. He lilted up at the end of every sentence, so the words hung in the air like a question. To my irritation, he also spoke very slowly, stretching out his vowels as long as possible. "When we aaaariiiiiiiiiiive at the time for praaaaaaayer, yoooooooooou may leeeeeeeead us?" After a while, I was fuming and tempted to yell at him, using some of my best profanity, to just move it along. I was stressed out, and we had things to do.

What Todd probably didn't know was that Tim and I had purposely arrived early for our appointment. We took a little self-guided tour of the casket showroom, or whatever that tastefully lit sales floor of $10,000 shiny boxes was called. Years later I would call it The Container Store and laugh and laugh. Our father had told us repeatedly over the years not to spend too much goddamn money on funeral stuff (it's a racket he said, like wedding dresses and extended warranties) so we circled the room until we saw the simple pine box in a back corner, unlit and unassuming. That was the one. He had requested to be cremated, so this wooden box was just for show at the visitation, anyway. It was all wood, so he could ride in it through the cremation.

Tim selected a nice urn—gray stone, heavy, in a trapezoid

shape. His ashes would be buried in Burnside Cemetery, next to my mom, and near my maternal grandparents.

In the conference room, the three of us finished up with the niceties and generalities. Todd stood up, and said he wanted to personally give us a tour through the "casket salon." Tim and I knew this was the next step because this was not our first encounter with this funeral home. We had been through this when our mother died a few years earlier, same funeral home but a different funeral director, and had a good idea of what would happen. The last time we saw our mother, she was in her rose-colored metallic box, head resting on a pink satin pillow, at the back of our Catholic church. No expense had been spared, under orders from our father. We had tucked a Harlequin Romance paperback and a pack of cigarettes under her arm, just before they closed the lid. We were going to put in a little bottle of booze and a lighter, but that could have gone badly, so we skipped them.

We followed Todd into the room. Before he could launch into his good/better/best sales pitch, we told him we had already made our selections and pointed them out. He pursed his lips, just a little, in a way that would have been adorable on a frustrated toddler. He made some notes on his clipboard. Todd told us that if we were planning to have an open casket visitation, our father had to be embalmed or, as he said, "preserved." That was fine. I am no dead body expert, but I think our father would have looked a little rough around the edges after just spending several days chilling in the fridge.

We went back to the conference room, and Todd opened several catalogs and binders, with a flourish. The first binder displayed our choices of programs for the service, with designs ranging from the cheapest, with lightweight white paper and tiny blue flowers, to the premier line, with heavy paper, a debossed image of Jesus himself, floating around on a cloud. I saw the prices and rolled my eyes at Tim. I smiled sweetly, and said, "Oh, we don't need programs, Todd, we're designing and printing them ourselves." More pursing, more notes on the clipboard. We also declined the business card-sized "remembrance cards." Such a thoughtful way to remind your friends, family, and loved ones of your father. We mentioned that our friends, family, and loved ones had many other ways to remember our father, and who he was. For better or worse. More notes. More clipboard. More pursing.

During the visitation, there would be music playing. Todd told us, "The appropriate music creates a soothing environment for mourners to pay their last respects to your loved one and the family." He listed off the categories of Christian hymns, harp music, soothing instrumentals, and Gregorian chants – all appropriate choices. Todd paused, his blue pen hovering over the clipboard, waiting for us to pick one. We had other ideas. We knew from our mother's service that we could provide our CDs, rather than pay to use their sad, sad music. The instrumentals were particularly bad. The gentle piano music and wailing violins reminded us of war widows getting bad news, or lonely lighthouse keepers at sunset. We said we had it covered. When he asked what we would be playing, we said Charlotte Church. Glenn Campbell. The Best of Johnny Cash. More pursing. A sigh. We knew our father was especially fond of "Ring of Fire" and would want us to play it. Looks would be exchanged, but we didn't care. Thinking about that song, I was having trouble keeping it together, and I couldn't look at Tim. I was scared of what unholy sound would fly out of me if I started to laugh and wondered if I would be able to stop. We filled out more forms and signed our names.

Finally, all we had left was the memorial service. Even though our father didn't want a funeral, we decided to have a short memorial at the end of the visitation. People in my small hometown expected it. They would come to pay their respects. We would invite a few friends and family to the cemetery, later in the week, post-cremation, to send our father off to the Big Car Show in the Sky. We worked our way through Todd's lengthy eulogy questionnaire. We checked the boxes and filled in some nouns and a bunch of adjectives. Our father was never a churchgoer, unless you counted when he was a teenager, and he and his buddies, the "Ratler boys" from down the road, picked up girls at the tent revivals in the Sandhills of Nebraska. We had heard stories of those revivals, likely heavily edited stories, from our father over the years.

Our father would get a simple service, no big speeches, no organ music, just quick and easy. We handed the completed questionnaire back to Todd, along with the obituary we had written for the local paper, and a photo. Todd pulled out a calculator and added up all the charges for the preservation, the pine box, the urn, the service, and the cremation, listed on his clipboard. He gave us a figure, and requested half the balance, with the other half due when our father's cremains were picked up. We wrote him a check.

The next day, our father's three siblings, two with spouses in tow, arrived from Alabama, Colorado, and California. Our father's small house was now full of opinionated old people, and they were shouting commands, like, "Don't throw away those books on tape, I want them!" and "Where does Mike keep the coffee filters?" Most of the shouting was because our father's older brothers, Jim and George, were hard-of-hearing, and stubbornly refused to wear hearing aids. My Aunt Karen groused, *those boys just vex me, I'm so tired of repeating myself.* I wondered what it was like, in the 1940s and 1950s, those four growing up together. We all settled into the task of the evening, gathering and choosing photos to be displayed at the wake. There were boxes of photos and albums to go through. Each potential photo choice would stir up a rush of commentary. "I remember that house," or "Woo, do you remember what our father did to Mike when he found out what he did? Now what was the name of that family down the road? That's a good photo of Mike and Margaret." The group was easily derailed, so we set a goal of finding ten or so photos that almost everyone could agree on. It took a long time, but we got it done.

There was also plenty of discussion about what to call the event, a wake or visitation. My family, probably because of Irish tradition on my mother's side, always called the gathering a wake, rather than a visitation. Though our father joked once, we're there to visit them, not wake them up.

On Thursday, Tim, Aunt Karen, and I drove to the funeral home downtown and dropped off the framed and unframed photos: Mike as a gas station attendant in the 1950s; Mike on a cruise ship with our mother; Mike getting business awards; Mike showing a fish he caught; Mike with his mother, eating a slice of her lemon pie; Mike in Jamaica, wearing a straw hat; and the one with our whole family, taken about five years earlier, when my son was only five, and our mother was still alive. Later in the afternoon, the family changed into our somber best, despite the heat, and headed back to the funeral home, mentally preparing ourselves for both our own emotions and the line of people who were sure to attend.

When we got to the funeral home, our father was on display in the place of honor, on a curtained stand at the front of the room. I busied myself with the photos on the table and admired the extraordinary number of flower arrangements, wreaths, and plants people had sent. There were so many they created a botanical U-shape around the room. When I ran out of things to organize, I finally made my way to the front of the room, along with Tim. Our father was ensconced in his pine box, fully embalmed, powdered, and rouged, so he resembled a somewhat solid, waxy version of himself. The last time I had seen our father, he had just expired. I had touched his face and held his hand. The last time I saw him, he was still warm. Seeing him in his pine box, there was a pronounced emptiness; his lifeforce, his vitalness, was long gone from this cool body. I leaned over and whispered something to him. Maybe I said that I loved him. Maybe I said goodbye. Tim and I cried. We must have. I was trying to block so many emotions, compartmentalize, and just make it through the day. I can't remember.

The visitation was much as we expected: a constant stream of mourners. Businesspeople from our small hometown; Catholic churchgoers, who had known my grandmother or my mother; current neighbors; old neighbors; relatives we had forgotten we had. There was the endless shaking of hands, many of them limp or clammy despite the heat; murmured condolences; the clunk of sympathy cards being deposited into the brass card box. A few people arrived with small gifts or photos of our father. Someone left us a chocolate cake, with brown frosting melting under the cellophane wrap.

By the end of the visitation, we were already exhausted as people took their seats in the brown chairs arranged in tight rows for the memorial service. With the microphoned podium in the front, the carefully arranged chairs, and the expectant faces, it looked like the stage was set for a lecture on British history or successful investment strategies. Everyone settled, the chatter slowly fizzled out, and finally, it was quiet. A Lutheran pastor who had never actually met our father would lead the celebration of life service. It should be noted that no one in the family was, or ever had been Lutheran. A few of us were Catholic, with the rest ranging from apathetic Christians to George, an insistent atheist. In my hometown, this was as close to nondenominal as we were going to get. The pastor had introduced himself to our family earlier, and there were handshakes all around. He said he had everything he needed, and it didn't occur to any of us to ask for a preview of the service.

The pastor started with a warm welcome and an opening prayer. Then he began to eulogize our father, Mike, with great enthusiasm, often referring to the questionnaire we had completed. Born in Nebraska, married in California, widower, two children, one grandson, and a granddaughter. And then things started going off the rails. Mike was a successful businessman here in town for over 25 years. But in his younger days, he managed a muffler shop, and before that, he was a cowboy, something he enjoyed very much.

My brother and I sat on hard chairs in the front row, sweating in the sticky heat from too many people and not enough AC. Tim and I stared straight ahead and did not dare look at each other. We bit the sides of our mouths so as not to snort on hearing our father described as a cowboy. Successful businessman, father, grandfather, cowboy! Sure, we know he rode horses on the ranch when he was a kid. But that was before he turned 15, was run over by a car in the Sandhills of Nebraska, and almost died.

Later in the service, after a reading from the book of John, the pastor was starting to wind up for the finale. Mike was certainly much beloved by his family and friends. He was many things to many people during his life. Father. Grandfather. Businessman. Cowboy. We could hear some snickering coming from the back, where Tim's friends were sitting.

During the final prayer, the lid was closed on that pine box, on our father, and this chapter of life. The finality of it all hit me. We stood up and spent the next 20 minutes mumbling, over and over, *thanks for coming*.

It had been a very long day, and we were tired and needed food. We drove through downtown, the six or eight of us, and seated ourselves at Liberty's, a local restaurant. We compared clammy handshakes, weird conversations, and alleged "memories" of our father, that we were pretty sure were not true. Thankfully, no one had insisted our father owed them money, was a long-lost relative, or a former spouse. Or girlfriend. Or son or daughter. Later, we howled with the laughter that only comes from pitchers of beer and recent death.

****

We started getting our father's affairs in order, though it would take months to organize everything. The morning our father would be laid to rest in the cemetery, Tim, along with our father's siblings Karen and George, drove downtown to the funeral home to pick him up. There were a couple of forms to sign and a check to write, and the urn containing our father was handed over to Tim. There were no instructions or specific protocol given on how to transport the urn home, so Tim buckled it in the backseat, right next to Uncle George. If George had thoughts about that, he didn't mention them. Once at the house, the urn sat on the kitchen table, until it was time to say our last goodbyes.

*****

Six days after our father died, he rode in his new yellow Corvette convertible for the first time. Tim had named it Big Mike, in honor of him. Our father had bought the car months before, "by accident" on eBay, but he had been too sick to drive it. Tim strapped him securely in the passenger seat, the gray urn heavy with ashes and symbolism. He drove him around town and down by the Mississippi, giving him the grand tour on his way to the cemetery. It was a steamy July day. The top was down. The sun was shining.

Tim arrived at the cemetery, carried the urn, and put it down in the grass, in front of the headstone. We were a small group—just our father's siblings, spouses, a few friends and their kids, my son Samson, and Tim and me. We stood and waited for someone to say something — we had been so focused on the visitation and other arrangements that we had not planned this part.

For a few minutes, we kicked at the stubby grass with our toes and watched cars drive by on the highway. The little ones ran between headstones and found bugs in the warm ground. Someone cleared their throat, maybe it was me (maybe not), and started a sentence with, *I remember.* At some point, I told the story about my father coming out to the driveway in his underwear with a shotgun, when I was 19. I had arrived home at 3:00am on the back of a Harley, surrounded by several more. My father didn't care that the guy, named Earl, was a friend of a friend and had bought me pancakes at Larry's Broiler before bringing me home.

As we shared our stories and laughed, we noticed the gravedigger, about 20 feet away, leaning on a golf cart, holding a shovel, and checking his watch. He was older, but of indeterminate age, his pale face tinged with gray. He had large ears and loose lips the color of raw liver. An unlit cigarette, no filter, dangled downward from one side of his mouth.

We continued to talk about my father until the torrent of stories became a trickle. We had been side-eying the gravedigger, willing him to leave, but he never abandoned his post. When there was finally a long pause in our storytelling, the gravedigger called out, "Are you folks about done? We got another one in ten minutes."

My brother and son Samson carefully placed the urn in the hole the size of two cereal boxes and said, "'Bye Dad. 'Bye Grandpa." I didn't say anything. We turned and walked away to let the gravedigger finish the job.

We got in our cars, seats sizzling in the midday sun. Most of us had driven to the cemetery in our muscle cars, sports cars, and convertibles. I drove the twinkly gold Trans Am I had inherited from my mother. We revved every engine and then lit up twelve smokey burnouts in tribute, our version of the 21-gun salute, as we left the cemetery. Big Mike led us down the highway.

That day thudded and echoed with finality. My brother and I were orphans, with Tim barely in his 30s. Everything left unsaid would have to remain unsaid. We always think we have more time. It's a cliché, but it's true. I would give up a lot to just have one more conversation with my father. I know so much more now than I did then. I'm so much healthier and aware. I would tell him I'm sorry. For letting him down. For expecting more than he could give. I know he did the best he could. It's probably too much to ask and too big of a risk to expect him to tell me he's proud of me. I have to be okay with filling that gap myself. I want him to know I turned out okay. We all did.

Jonni Lynn

In October 2019, my sister drove away, in an early-season snowstorm, and I never saw her again.

Jonni was my half-sister I didn't know I had. From that first shocking message on Ancestry.com to that last breathy phone call, I knew her for 33 months, 3 weeks and 4 days. Her father was my father. We were seven years apart. She was the older sister, and for a time in our childhoods, we lived within 20 miles of one another in California. We had the same beaky nose and pointy chin, and with her high cheekbones, she was the spitting image of our grandmother, Merna, in photos in her younger days.

My father was barely 20 when Jonni was born, and Jonni's mother was 17. It was unclear if my father ever knew about the baby. During the pregnancy or shortly after, he quit his job at the service station, and moved more than 100 miles away. Jonni's mother insisted for decades that our father was a shit heel who intentionally abandoned her and Jonni. Maybe he did or maybe he didn't. My father had died 20 years before I got the first message from Jonni, my mother three years before him. There is no one left to ask, no tools to excavate the truth.

Jonni was a double-lung transplant recipient, and more than anything, she had a ferocious curiosity about the medical history on her father's side. Maybe about her father, in general. For decades, all she had to go on was a name, spat like a curse, the name of that boy, that man, really, with the black hair and green eyes, Jonni's mother had met in California in the late 50s.

Jonni scoured phone books, and whatever research materials she could find at the library. She even hired a private detective in the early 90s, before the Internet could help. Jonni was born in California, and focused her search there, not knowing that her biological father had married, had two more children, and left the state in the early 1970s. He had put down new roots to grow his family tree in the practical and conservative Midwest. Jonni had also left and moved to Kansas with her mother. Two more sisters came along, and her mother's various boyfriends and husbands drifted in and out of the picture. Money was always tight, and Jonni said her mother turned a blind eye to the late-night activities of the men who financially supported her and her girls. Things were bad for Jonni for a lot of her childhood. We had that in common. Jonni moved to Florida as an adult. She married late in life and did not have children.

The story of Jonni and me started in October of 2018 when I got a message on Ancestory.com from a woman who said she thought we were cousins. That was very hard to believe, as I only had a total of four biological cousins, across two sets of aunts and uncles, and I knew them all. My other two cousins were adopted. Uncle George was a wildcard, but by then we knew he was a gay man, and had passed away from complications of AIDS, another family secret that came to light after his death.

In the back of my mind, I just knew this woman was running a scam, and I waited to see what she was after – money, probably. I answered the first message, aloof, clear in my eye-rolling disbelief. Another message followed, then another. Maybe we are related in another way, the woman said. A cousin at least, she insisted, or some other type of close relative. I was steadfast in my skepticism. Finally, we agreed we would both do a test on 23&Me. This second DNA test would confirm what she was insisting was true, she said. Ten days later, the test results came back: 28% shared DNA. We weren't cousins, we were sisters. Actual sisters, well, half-sisters. Google told me that typical half-siblings share 25% of DNA. The data left no doubt.

I was shocked. I was obsessed. I was so angry with my father for being careless, and for never telling me. And it was so frustrating, the fact that it was impossible to unleash my fury on a ghost. Instead, I stuffed it all inside, where it burned brightly.

I called my brother, and he was shaken but not completely surprised – he was the one holding his breath when we placed the notice in the newspaper when our father died. Deep down, I think he understood more about my father than I ever did. I called my aunt in Alabama, who was closest to my father. Did she know? This was news to everyone, and the first question was, What does she want? Money? We are a truly suspicious bunch.

Emails with Jonni led to phone calls. Jonni, like my mother, like my Aunt Karen, could talk for a very, very long time. Without taking a breath, it seemed. Without noticing that I had not said a word. After one particular two-hour marathon call, I told her I just had to hang up. That my phone was out of battery. It was a lot. She was a lot. I didn't tell her that part. Jonni was intense, bossy, opinionated, and a somewhat aggressive extrovert, but I didn't care. I now had a sister.

    She emailed me pictures of herself. I did the same, and finally sent some of my father. That made her cry, she said. She never said if it was out of relief, gratitude, or something else completely. After a couple of weeks of these intense exchanges and long conversations with my husband and my brother, I decided to get on a plane to Orlando and go see her in person. "You'll regret it if you don't," they said. It was quite a weekend.

    My entire life, I had wanted a sister. Before my brother was born, I was banking on a girl, and obviously was disappointed. In elementary school, I envied my friends with sisters. The closeness, the acceptance, the sharing, being part of something. Sisterhood. Security. What came as a surprise to me, as an adult, I again longed for a sister, to have another woman in the family I could relate to, count on, really talk to, and perhaps, after all this time, not feel so alone as I age. My husband is amazing and supportive but in a very male, masculine way. He's an engineer, a fixer, and that is not always what I need. Sometimes "female stuff" and talking about feelings, on the rare occasions I do, leaves him feeling out of his depth and confused. He tries his best. I am very different from both of my sisters-in-law and while they are both very nice, I failed to make a close connection with either of them, even after nearly 20 years of being part of their family. So, after learning I had a sister, and that I've always had a sister, I was ready to embrace sisterhood with all I had. I was going to Orlando, and it was going to be the best weekend ever. I was determined.

After arriving in Orlando, I quickly discovered Jonni only had one button – ON – one volume – LOUD – and one speed – FAST–. Jonni was as impulsive, rowdy, over-the-top, pushy, and without boundaries, as I was the opposite. I think at one point, she called me a little mouse. Case-in-point: We went to dinner at a Brazilian place in Orlando that was famous for its dinner and dancing show. After we ordered drinks, Jonni popped up and smiled at me. Before I knew what was happening, she beelined it to the large table next to us, where a family was celebrating someone's birthday. It was very loud in the restaurant, so I couldn't hear what she was saying to the man at the head of the table. But I could see her pointing at me, excitedly, and talking to the man. He nodded and smiled politely, and Jonni walked back to our table and sat down, letting her trademark cackle fly.

"What was that all about?" I asked her.

"Oh, I just told that guy that you're my sister, and we just found out about each other, and he should buy us a drink to celebrate!" I was mortified. She thought it was hilarious. Later in the evening, the DJ announced that anyone having a birthday or celebration should come up on the stage, and share it with the audience. Preteens with their moms and couples who were celebrating an anniversary started to line up. Jonni shoved her chair back, and before I could ask her what she was doing, she fast-walked to the end of the line near the stage and waited her turn with the microphone. Luckily, for me at least, the DJ took back the mic while there were still several people in line in front of Jonni. She came back to the table, obviously disappointed.

During that weekend, Jonni also talked me into ziplining and crossing the suspension bridges at Gatorland. Despite me telling her about my suspension bridge fears, she gleefully jumped up and down and shook the ropes, as I slowly made my way across the expanse, dozens of sleepy alligators and crocodiles roaming and sunning themselves fifty feet beneath me. I clutched the ropes, lagging far behind her. I was near tears, and she was having a great time, joking with the staff, and trying to get them to shake the ropes with her. When I mentioned this at the end of the day, she told me she was sorry, but with a gleam in her eye and a little smirk. She told me I needed to loosen up a little. Maybe that was true.

The following year, Jonni got a new car and planned a cross-country road trip. She was eerily like our father in this way, looking for an excuse to hit the road. She was always up for an adventure. Not to mention, a meal and a quick shopping trip at Cracker Barrel. As she made her way north, Jonni said she wanted to stop by and see us. We had been in our new house less than a month, but we got the guest room set up for her. She brought in her suitcase, along with a nearly equal-sized case containing her antirejection and other meds. It hadn't occurred to me what she needed to do to keep her donor lungs safe and healthy. We went out for a nice dinner that first night and my husband finally got to meet her in person. She was a little more subdued than I remember, but I chalked it up to long days of driving. She spent the next two days holed up in the guest room and the bathroom, suffering from either the flu or food poisoning. I kept her supplied with Sprite, Kleenex, and crackers. By the third day, she felt much better and was itching to get back on the road. I loaded her up with snacks, and we prepared to say our goodbyes. When we stepped outside, it had started to snow. Big, thick, slushy flakes that turned the neighborhood into a suburban snow globe. Jonni was absolutely delighted. My husband Steve, the engineer, the brother-in-law she didn't know she had, helped Jonni clear the snow off the car, and offered her one of our extra snowbrushes. She and I had one long, hard hug before she climbed into the car. With a smile and a wave, and a beep of the horn, she was gone.

    Over the next couple of years, we liked each other's posts on Facebook and emailed and texted once in a while. I feel guilty now saying that I intentionally kept her at arm's length, while she was seeking a deeper relationship. My therapist said that guilt is a useless emotion, but I don't know that I agree. I think sometimes we need to feel just bad enough to force us to process things that have happened. Self-forgiveness has never been one of my strong traits.

In 2021, Jonni was struck with an illness that hospitalized her repeatedly and baffled the doctors. Everyone prayed her body was not rejecting her donor lungs. They ruled out dozens of diagnoses, the last one being Legionnaire's Disease. Eventually, her body and her lungs started to give up and shut down. We were in Iceland that July and Jonni was getting sicker. She texted me more than once, asking me to call her. And I didn't. I said I would call her when we got home. I feel ashamed now. I really do. I didn't understand how ill she was. All I could think about was having an hour-long or longer conversation with her during our vacation. Hearing, "I know, right?!" over and over and over. I didn't want to make the time. I would do it later. We got home, and for the first few days, I forgot.

Then, a text: renee can i call you.

I sighed. I texted back, that was fine, but in an hour, after my conference call. She called, and right away, I was shocked at the slowness of her words, the weakness, the breathiness of her voice. The doctors were letting her go, she said. Nothing was working. They had run out of ideas. And she wanted to talk to me one last time, hear my voice, say goodbye. The conversation went on for a long time, punctuated by silences and her quiet wheezing. I told her I had written a poem about us, and she wanted to read it. I sent it to her, and I asked if I should come down to Florida. She said no. I missed my next meeting, and the one after that. We continued to talk, with her husband, Marshall interjecting, at times. Punching through the silence.

Then she said, "I have a big favor to ask, Sis." Since I was a writer, she wanted me to write a Facebook post - part obituary, part urgent notice to her Facebook friends - that she was dying. In it, she wanted me to emphatically stipulate to her friends DON'T SEND THOUGHTS/ BLESSINGS/PRAYERS OR ANY OF THAT BULLSHIT. The conversation had turned surreal, a little wild, and 100% Jonni. Her wish, she said, was that she could read the nice things her friends were going to write about her before she passed. I did what she asked. Within an hour, I had feverishly written a post that was part funny, part wistful, part tribute, part goodbye. I sent it to her to approve. Marshall said she loved it. I posted it, and her friends on Facebook responded with waves of love and kindness. Marshall read every response to her. "She was so happy," he said. I told Marshall to tell her hi for me, but no hugs. I'm not a damn hugger. He said that made her laugh. A few days later, she was gone. In the end, I didn't think to tell her goodbye. We had parted with, "See you later!"

Jonni was an unexpected last link to my father. She swept through my life like a loud song in a foreign language. I was not sure what to make of her, or what she thought of me. And now, in the silence, I'm unsure how to grieve her loss. It's like holding sorrow in one hand and joy in the other.

While Jonni wasn't exactly what I envisioned or what I thought I needed from a sister I never knew I had, maybe our time together served a need for each of us. She showed me what I might have been like if my life had been different. I could have been more extroverted, joyful, less cautious, and wary. I'm not sure I could ever match her intensity, but I did learn that I could just tell people to fuck right off when necessary without worrying about offending them. That it was okay to protect myself because no one was doing it for me. I could be selfish sometimes.

My gift to her was sharing photos and memories of our father and writing that obituary post. So she could hear about the difference she made in people's lives, especially others with organ transplants, and she could feel the warmth of other's love for her. I will always feel good about that. Happy trails, Jonni. Until we meet again.

POSTCARDS FROM THE ROAD: PART II

Angels in Plaid Shirts

Thank you, Angels.

Twenty miles outside Sidney, Nebraska, I heard the thump, thump of a tire that was breathing its last, leaving its skin in the right lane of I-80, and its bones on the wheel. It was January, and I was leaving Minnesota in the rearview and heading to Albuquerque. I was a mid-year transfer student to the University of New Mexico, and it was time to go. I was both driving toward my future and away from something else. Away from a lot of things. I had made mistakes, and I had put myself in danger – real danger – more than once. In the previous two-and-a-half years, I had been battered and nearly destroyed by two separate assaults, and I lost the scholarship I needed to stay at the Catholic college I attended in northern Minnesota. I made terrible choices in men, money, and alcohol. I had recently come home from studying abroad in Ireland, and during the last couple of months I was there, I got engaged to a boy, and then we broke up. It was messy, and I felt lost.

When I got back from Ireland, Duluth had gotten too small, too cold, too provincial for me, and I needed a change. There were too many people I knew, and too many places that held very bad memories. I fired off applications to colleges in warm places that I could sort of afford. I was accepted by Arizona State, the University of Texas at Austin, and the University of New Mexico. New Mexico was the cheapest. I prepared for a new start in the desert.

I didn't know a soul in Albuquerque, and that was okay with me. The inside of my 1976 Plymouth Duster was packed to the rafters with pots and pans, clothes, and my Smith Corona typewriter, hefty in its light blue case. The trunk of the Duster was a treasure trove of shoes, frying pans, and bedding in white garbage bags, anchored by my 50-pound RCA television.

I had been fiddling with the radio, trying to find the sweet spot between Jesus and Dolly Parton, when I heard that sound and felt the pull of the wheel. I had been on the road for hours that day, driving by dormant cornfields with their lonely stubby stalks, waving at truckers, and eating gas station doughnuts. I was trying to make it to my grandmother's house in Fort Morgan, Colorado, for lemon cake pie, homemade biscuits, and easy games of cards. I confidently flew by every exit for Grand Island, Nebraska, where my family usually stopped, with the hubris that only a 20-year-old can possess.

I pulled over on the shoulder and stopped. This was years before cell phones. If I got out, that flat tire was going to be real. I thought I would just sit for a minute. I hummed along to Led Zeppelin on the radio. Ate a chocolate-covered donut. That minute turned into five and I finally clicked out of my seatbelt and opened the door. Yep, the left rear tire, flatter than flat and missing several layers of rubber. I knew how to change a tire – my father wouldn't let me out in the world without it. We had practiced and practiced when I got my driver's license at 16. By practice, I mean my father stood in the driveway, in his baggy jeans, plaid shirt, and cardigan, smoking a cigarette. He pointed out where I missed something, very occasionally telling me, that was pretty good. I knew where to locate the jack, I knew how to loosen lug nuts, and I could heft the spare out of the trunk. I knew what to do.

I opened the trunk and sighed. It had taken two of us, my father and I, to get that huge RCA television into the trunk. There is no way one of me was going to hoist it out. And the spare tire, which we had checked just two days before, was tucked in its compartment under everything. I looked to the freeway, and there were no cars for several flat miles, in either direction.

More sighing.

I started unloading the trunk on the side of the road. Comforters. Shoes. A spare winter coat. My red Slimline telephone. I dug and lifted until nothing was left in the cavernous space but that damn RCA. I rocked it one way and then the other. There was just no way I could get it out. I stood with my hands on my hips. I was a 20-year-old girl with no more good ideas.

I turned toward the freeway. I heard the distant rumble of 18 wheels eating the road. Long before I saw it. I had no choice. I flapped my right hand listlessly. I tried hard to look brave and tough and not cry. Tried not to think about the fact that I could be kidnapped right there by the side of the road, or murdered. My picture and story would end up on 48 Hours, for sure. The mountain of a vehicle started to slow, edging toward the shoulder, and came to a stop with a whoosh of air brakes. The driver, with his straw hat, cowboy boots, brown suspenders, and round belly, stepped down from the truck cab. He was as old as my dad, sun-soaked and strong. "Looks like you have a problem there, little lady." Without permission, two tears wobbled down my face as he approached me. He hitched up his jeans. "Let's see what we got."

He helped me yank that TV out of the trunk like a tooth from a socket. We grabbed the spare tire and the jack and got to work. I jacked up the car, and he unscrewed the lug nuts. One was very stubborn and he swore at it with great creativity and enthusiasm. We pulled that tire off, and as we did, the rest of the rubber shrugged off the rim onto the ground. We put the wheel, its once-shiny surface now pitted and scratched, on my front seat, and loaded everything back into the trunk. He got on his CB and found out good news and bad. The good news was there was a garage 20 miles away, in Sidney, and they could get me a tire. The bad news was that they would get it tomorrow. Or the next day. He told them I was coming.

I thanked him and offered him ten dollars for helping me, but he laughed and told me to spend it on a new tire. I pulled back on the interstate, and drove far slower than the posted speed, with the radio off, straining to hear any signs of distress from the spare tire. There was honking, as I was passed by every car and truck heading in the same direction. I made it to Sidney. I found the garage and pulled a third of my cash out of my red wallet to pay George the mechanic for the new tire. I left my car and most of my possessions in his care. I stayed overnight a few blocks away in a Howard Johnson's Motor Inn, with the dresser pushed in front of the door. When I walked back to the garage early the next afternoon, the tire had arrived. George clearly felt sorry for me. "Hey, I got a kid your age." He didn't charge me to remove the spare and tuck it back into the compartment in the trunk, next to the jack, under the bags of bedding, and the RCA. George said that damn TV weighed 60 pounds.

I made it to Fort Morgan, a day late. I stopped overnight, ate two good meals, and was sent on my way in the morning, with a lemon cake pie and a plastic fork. From Fort Morgan, it was about an eight-hour drive to Albuquerque. I arrived right before the sun was thinking of setting over the mesa, and there was just enough golden hour left to read the street signs. I already had my key, so I hauled everything out of the Duster and up to my apartment until nothing remained but the TV. I stood in the parking lot, in the deep twilight, and assumed the hands-on-hip position, as I stared into the trunk. An angel, in the shape of a plaid-shirted man named Terry Garcia (or that's the name he gave me, anyway), asked me if I needed some help. Together, slowly, we carried that TV from the parking lot up the stairs to my second-floor studio apartment. The next morning, I wanted to thank him. I described him to the apartment manager. She said that no one named Terry Garcia lived there. I never saw him again.

I was not prone to thinking about God, about angels, about mysterious, mystical protectors. I attended Mass when required by family obligation, I lit candles in church because the ritual was comforting. But my hard-edged cynicism about religion, about those all-powerful beings who supposedly lived in the clouds, who controlled what happened to me in everyday life, had begun to seep in. It all started to make less sense than when I blindly accepted it earlier in my life. All the dogma, the unlikely-to-be-true Biblical myths I absorbed during five years of Catholic school, two years of confirmation classes and then Catholic college. I mean, didn't God control the hands of the men who wrote the Bible? Whispered in their ears, shared the Truth™, the Good News, His word, to control the people? But I digress.

Maybe a benevolent God, a personal savior did not, could not exist. I was starting to think that maybe this patriarchal God was just not for me. Maybe I just had "daddy issues." How would this Father God explain sitting on the sidelines while I experienced such horrible, evil things? I was sad and angry and I wanted answers. But at that point, I didn't have anything better to replace Christianity, Catholicism so I continued to search. I wanted to believe so badly.

Sing Your Hymn of the Open Road

To My Father:

    The maroon convertible was all winged fenders and pin tucking, a glossy angel dropped from the Corvette heavens of Bowling Green. Glass-pack pipes murmured and growled like Leonard Cohen in his later years. That car, that sound, even that color heralded your arrival at every stoplight, summoning your acolytes to point and stare. Flags waved and marching bands played. You probably thought they were for you.

    The convertible top was down and you smiled, so benevolent. You were fatherly, for just a moment. To me, that chrome, those pipes, only signaled leaving. I saw what you couldn't: When you inserted the key in the ignition and turned it over, you reanimated. Your face relaxed, and you were happy, even, in a way you couldn't even pretend to be when you were here. How could a daughter compete with that Siren call of the open road?

    You scorched the newborn grass at the side of the driveway, lifting and pressing your brown booted foot on the accelerator, your movements rhythmic, tense, masculine. As you revved that engine, it was a racehorse waiting, impatient to be released to the freedom of the track. You gave life to every piston, and the RPMs leaped and fell at your command. Unlike you, the gauges told no lies.

    It was quieter, after that final crescendo, and the shiny pipes barely quivered.

You gestured to me with a few fingers above the steering wheel, halfway between a salute and a wave. Then you shifted the gears and began to reverse, slowly, a hand flung over the back of the passenger seat, your head turned away from me. Words fluttered in your breeze.

How did I consider you – when you drove off the long side of the map? I asked the robins singing their cheerful tune above me, but they forgot how to carry that tune. The leaving song. Just as you forgot the concept of me, of what it meant to be home. Family. You were far too restless to ponder such things. And wishing got me nowhere. You and your machine devoured the highways, swaying to the two-part harmony of hypnotic thumps and hum of rubber-eating asphalt. I immersed myself in books, seeking hidden messages and obscure answers from explorers like you. But there are some roads even words cannot hope to travel.

Leaving is What We Do

Dear Husband:

We found each other later in life, completely by accident. When I met you, I didn't even like you very much. I thought you were boorish. You thought I was flaky. We were both bruised by divorce and were carrying messy and overflowing bags from those first marriages. But somehow, we clicked. We thought, what if?

And then you, my love, and I became terrible at goodbyes. We part like tearing Velcro, fiber by fiber, loudly, gripped. Like stripping a first name from the last. That summer night at the park was unexpected. When we were new. We leaned against my red car and kissed like teenagers. Curious. Focused. Not caring who saw us. We peeled apart only as the sprinklers, dozens of them in sequence, popped and hissed, arcing. We were just close enough to the grass that we were pelted in a watery rhythm. We struggled to close the convertible top and laughed, more panicked than gleeful.

The water silvered under the sodium lights, soaking the warm air with minerals and the smell of wet dogs and earth. We sat in the car, dripping, panting from effort, lit only by the dull lights on the dash. We said nothing, as the windshield fogged, and encased us in a blanket of closeness. You looked toward your car, in the middle distance. You turned to me, and for a horrible moment, I thought you were going to shake my hand. You cleared your throat and said, "I really like you, you know." I nodded. I waited for more, but there was nothing. My tongue remained still in my mouth, my throat a dam of sawdust. You said, "Okay, then. I'll call you." You opened the car door, while I watched you with such fragile longing. I thought I'd crack into shards when you slammed it closed. I realized then what I wanted to say was, *wait*. I realized I wanted to say, stay with me. Instead, I said, *goodbye*... to an empty car, humid air, your broad back.

It would be months before I was brave enough to speak any of those things to you without holding my breath for a response. Even longer for me to blurt out that I loved you. That night, the best I could do was call out... *goodbye*.

Apologies To My Body (As a Vehicle)

Dear Body:

 Look at you. You're my one and only vehicle. You were once brand new, delivered pink and precious, right from the factory. Maybe even a special order. Some would say you are my first love, but I'm not sure that's true at all. You're trusty, getting us from one place to another, usually. You're the place to park my head, because we both know I'm all thoughts and memories these days, and following directions has never really been my thing. As we traveled through life, your wheels rolled under me, propelling us forward. To the next adventure or terror or joy or just a fork in the road. You're my daily driver, the grocery getter, the one I can count on, even when times are bad. Like, really bad. You've been wobbly, you've slid, you've spun, every bit out of control. Your wheels have fallen off, and you've been so out of alignment, I haven't known where we were going or why. Or if we would even make it.

 Your chassis is covered with the thinnest veil of skin, and no one would ever accuse you of being top-of-the-line, at least not anymore. Maybe thirty years ago, when you were still shiny and sparkling and you didn't even know it. In fact, you're pretty banged up now, but I'll never trade you in. You are high-milage, but as my father would say, "You're a real good runner." Your exterior is scuffed, and of indeterminate color now. It used to be a perfect shade of tan that looked bronze and supple in the summer sunlight.

Now it bears the aftermath of bad decisions and scars from the war with my younger self, and the sun. Icarus and I used to be friends you know. Now we're just frenemies, and we only keep in touch on Facebook. Body, you're pale, you're faded and spotty, but you are still here. And for that, I suppose I should be grateful.

Body, when I close my eyes, I want to see the reflection of our many travels, in what's left of your finish. I really do. Every deep scar, pock, and stretch mark gauged in the hood, the river of healed stitches scratched into your doors. The window that refuses to open. The vestiges of long-ago accidents, collisions with solid objects we didn't see in time. I couldn't fix your damage until I had time and money. I'm sorry it took so long. Your replacement parts were never quite as good as the factory originals. I'm sorry. I did my best.

On the outside, you looked passable for years and years, and for the longest time, no one knew you were being held together with Bondo and gray primer, and slowly dissolving, as the rust gobbled up your insides. Until we made it stop. I want to see my history reflected in you – I do. I want to be reminded of the roads we've traveled, by choice or by circumstance. I have days, weeks even, where I can only see blackness or the emptiness of dense fog in the rearview. I want to know everything that happened to you, to us. But I haven't been able to look at you with that type of scrutiny, body. I just can't. The reports I have are from other people and places, and they only give facts about what happened after. How I was after. There are no credible witnesses.

I have to confess something to you, body: I have hated you. I mean, really hated you. But it's not your fault. Things were done to us that left us unable to love.

I'm sorry for so many things, body. I tried to save myself, over the years, in the only ways I knew how. To quiet your rattling, I drove and drove and drove and left your engine dry. You seized up and stalled. I didn't care. I cut you, first in tiny, hidden places, then out in the open, where everyone could see, but no one ever did. I hungered for attention and excitement, and you bore the brunt of what happened next. I almost got us killed, twice. Four times, if you count the times I tried to do it myself. I could only take so much.

Even with those bad decisions, we had some good times on the road, body. You have to admit, the 80's were fun, though 1988 may have been a bit extra. I'm sorry.

Body, I've been distracted. I have ignored you, your maintenance, your warning lights, sometimes on purpose. I could not bear to look at you or touch you. I couldn't go there with you, I just couldn't. Recently, I learned that not all weight is physical, and that made me pause.

Today, my head is clear, full of purpose. It's taken time, so much time, years on my journey, our journey, but I feel so new, so ready. I see your floorboards are decaying, your wheel wells collapsing. I'm not surprised, but I am sad. I hope I can save you. I am sorry for so many things, body. Please forgive me. Let me drive us home.

TRUE NORTH

Waffle House Redemption

I hadn't seen my daughter, Sarah, for more than four years. At least 2,400 miles, a global pandemic, and a new boyfriend had come between us since I saw her last, at that filthy sober living house in Los Angeles. That was a terrible visit, and it was obvious that she was in real trouble. The barrier between her and me had never been more resolute, and impenetrable, and my powerlessness to help her had never been more acute. When my brother Tim and I drove away that last afternoon, I felt less relieved to have seen her in person, and more like I was grieving in advance.

When I got home, I kept my phone on at night, next to the bed, anticipating the phone call that the waiting nightmare was over, and a new wound would be opened. The daughter I knew was already gone, and had been for several years. When the phone rang, I would need to identify the body.

And then, Sarah had emerged in Florida. There was a period of relative calm, and over a couple of years, there had been a thawing of sorts. She said she was clean and sober, and I had been working to exchange my anger for empathy. We were both maybe, finally in a place where we could pull ourselves out of our pain, and wanted to try to connect.

I asked Tim to come along to Jacksonville, as a buffer, as a distraction, as a physical and emotional navigator. Jacksonville was hot, even in early November. That weekend was Sarah's 27th birthday. I considered the fact that I had not celebrated a birthday with her since she turned 21, when we got a suite at the smoky Indian casino hotel in Minnesota. She and her friend went to the Thunder Down Under show. Sarah drank too much and spent much of the night throwing up. Our fancy Sunday brunch was a bust, and she was edgy and aggressive. After three stints in rehab for alcohol and opioids, she was in the vicious jaws of active heroin addiction that weekend, and I didn't know she was suffering from withdrawal. She was suffering. I understand far more now than I did then. That Sunday morning, I was just irritated that all the planning and money for her birthday weekend was going to waste. We sniped at each other across the breakfast table, as she tried to choke down some toast. I look back now on that day and feel stupid and embarrassed. I was naïve, and I felt like I was a terrible mother. I should have seen the signs. I should have tried harder to rescue her. But, at that point, she had very little interest in us being together, much less being rescued by me, or anyone.

    Sarah's birthmother used drugs and alcohol when she was pregnant and Sarah was prenatally exposed, permanently altering her brain development. Sarah spent some of her early life living in a meth lab in a Red Roof Inn motel. Her birthparents were arrested in a raid and went to prison for manufacturing drugs and child endangerment when Sarah was two years old. Sarah was there, at the raid, and hid with her birthmother in an abandoned bus, until police dogs tracked them, and pulled them out. After she went to prison, Sarah's birthmother would not relinquish her parental rights for nearly two years, selfishly dooming Sarah to the endless churn of the foster care system. When she came to us, at the age of three-and-a-half, we were Sarah's 12th placement. With no one to safely attach to, her brain had never developed the ability to form healthy bonds and relationships, and she was diagnosed with severe attachment disorder by the time she was six years old, two-and-a-half years after we adopted her.

It was no surprise, then, partly due to her attachment disorder, partly to preserve her addiction, Sarah was highly skilled at driving wedges between all of us, triangulating, manipulating. By her 21st birthday, she only had enough energy to feed her addiction, and enough love to give heroin, which she could not live without. After that birthday weekend, we never spent more than an hour or two together, at a time.

I had approached this trip to Jacksonville with caution. Sarah had finally been doing well, really well. She was living with her boyfriend Ty in their first apartment. She was very slowly working toward a two-year degree in nursing and was only a month away from completing her studies. Part of me could not be prouder, and I couldn't wait to see her, tell her that. Part of me was terrified that seeing me would somehow put her success in jeopardy. That it would be too much. But at least via text messages, in the weeks leading up to the visit, Sarah seemed excited I was coming. I was going to let Tim be a surprise guest.

Ty and Sarah suggested we meet at one of the museums in Jacksonville. We would meet in the afternoon, in front of the museum. I was chattering along to Tim about nothing, yammering, feeling the anxiety bubbling around in my body. My fist was clenched in a pocket full of feelings. Tim saw Sarah walking up the sidewalk before I did. His face changed, and I turned. She had grown her hair long and she was heavier than the last time I saw her. I thought she looked pretty. Her forehead was crinkled in stress, and I could see her tightly clutching Ty's hand. She was just as nervous as I was. We plastered smiles on our faces and hugged. It was quick, and I could smell her flowery shampoo. She seemed happy to see me, and thrilled to see Tim. The museum was silent and sparse; we only stayed for half an hour. They suggested we go to a second museum, and it was expansive. We spent two hours viewing the art and touring the gardens along the rolling James River. I was still nervous, but it seemed to go well, at least according to Tim, as I checked and whispered with him about every 15 minutes. I didn't trust myself to reliably read the room.

After the museums, we agreed to meet for dinner at a pizza place near our hotel.

I could tell Sarah was saturated in anxiety, facing the intensity of togetherness, of the four of us at a small wooden table. She was all over the place in the conversation, and could not decide what she wanted on her pizza, and finally resorted to listing the ingredients in her phone, and reading them out to the waiter. She had selected more than a dozen items, and before I could stop myself, I blurted, "Geez, Sarah! That's a thirty-dollar pizza!" Her face fell, and I could see her withdrawing. *Shit, shit,* I thought to myself. *That was the wrong thing to do. To say. It's not like I can't afford it*, I berated myself. *Had I learned nothing? Had I not learned how to fight my battles, what hills to die on? What the hell was wrong with me?*

The rest of the dinner went fine, with everyone sticking to safe topics, like the weather, food, and Sarah's impending nursing pinning ceremony, which I learned is like a graduation. We were going to miss the ceremony, as she had told us the wrong date initially, and five of us were already booked on a trip in December to the Dominican Republic. I hadn't told her yet. This trip was my peace offering. It was to be a celebration of her birthday, sure, but deep down, it was also driven by my guilt. I had so much.

We discussed what to do the next day, Sarah's birthday, before we went to a fancy celebratory dinner. Tim, the most enthusiastic driver among us, suggested a road trip to Savannah. It was only a little more than two hours away. We talked some more and agreed to pick them up at 8am for breakfast at Waffle House. Ty lived most of his 27 years in Florida, without ever having been to a Waffle House, which Tim and I thought was a crime. Waffle House was a delicious novelty for us, as they stopped popping up along the interstate somewhere in Missouri, some 300 miles south of us. Sarah had never been to a Waffle House, either. We went our separate ways after dinner. Later that night, Sarah texted she was sorry about the pizza, and I texted I was sorry about getting on her case.

Later, another text from Sarah, suggested we go to Darien, Georgia instead. It was an important location in the Civil War, and she and Ty wanted to see it. And, it was only an hour away from Jacksonville. Less time in the car with us, I supposed.

The next morning, we rolled up to their apartment building, in a less desirable part of Jacksonville than they had been led to believe when they rented the apartment. They had only lived there seven months but were already itching to get out. Between broken water pipes, a bathroom that flooded multiple times, and the amount of crime taking place in the parking lot, they were counting the days until Sarah could get a job as a nurse, and they could move.

In the spirit of any good road trip, we kept our eyes out for anything weird, or touristy. We saw sign after sign for the Florida Citrus Center, which reminded me of the Wall Drug signs along the interstate when I was a kid. We had to go. We were promised a huge display of citrus, the biggest alligator in Florida, and saltwater taffy, and the experience was only slightly disappointing. The Florida Citrus Center looked suspiciously like a former Sinclair gas station. When we walked in, the building smelled syrupy, and earthy from fresh pecans in bags, mixed with a tangy, green, aquatic smell of a huge aquarium filled with murky water and tiny baby alligators, crawling over each other, in search of food and freedom. The promised giant alligator was stuffed and perched dustily in a corner. We took selfies with it.

We had fun looking at all the tchotchkes, the key chains, the misspelled t-shirts, and coffee mugs. Bees were everywhere, especially near the tasting stations for the fresh-squeezed orange juice. I bought a bag of pecans, and we left, eager to get back on the road and breakfast.

We crossed the border into Georgia and easily found the first Waffle House. The restaurant was pretty clean, as I keep telling people most of them are, and the server was friendly. When she found out it was Sarah's birthday, she procured a paper Waffle House hat and made sure Sarah plopped it on her head. Sarah liked her waffle, and Ty devoured a huge breakfast. Bellies full, we hopped back into the rental car and headed deeper into Georgia. We cajoled Sarah into keeping her hat on.

As we rolled into Darien, population 1,500, we realized we had lucked out. The entire town was setting up for its annual fall festival. We maneuvered around the food trucks, white, pop-up tents, and families with blankets and coolers, as we made our way to Fort King George and a dose of Civil War history far removed from what we have in Minnesota. After a couple of hours of exploring the fully restored fort, we were ready for lunch and a different kind of culture. We drove back into downtown Darien, where the festival was in full swing. We found a place to park and followed the signs to the car show. It was impressive for such a tiny town, and we enjoyed the quality and variety of the vehicles and rolled our eyes, or at least, I did, at the number of Confederate flags proudly painted, stuck on, or flying on the trucks. Honestly, though, there were fewer than I expected.

We treated Ty to his first-ever funnel cake, and Sarah regaled him with the food experiences at the Minnesota State Fair and deep-fried everything. They met a local painter and bought two pictures from him. Full of sugar and sunshine, we drove back to Jacksonville.

When Sarah and Ty walked into the restaurant for her birthday dinner, I felt a little catch in my throat. Sarah looked so, well, healthy. Her hair was shiny, her face was sprinkled with freckles and she looked luminous. It was cute how she and Ty huddled together, deciding what they would eat for dinner, and she was thrilled at how many nonalcoholic drinks were available. She had told us at the pizza place that she didn't drink anymore and hadn't for more than two years. Dinner was good, and the conversation and laughs came easily. Anyone observing us would have thought it had always been that way. The waitress brought a dessert with a candle, and we sang Happy Birthday, off-key and enthusiastically. Driving back to the hotel after dinner, Tim and I talked about how good Sarah looked, and holy hell, how different the visit was.

The next morning, we met for breakfast near the hotel,

before Tim and I had to leave. We sat near the window and saw a middle-aged man back up his white Bentley, nearly popping over the curb and into the building, and get his to-go breakfast order. Joking about it helped pass the time. After breakfast, we said our goodbyes in the parking lot. We hugged, really hugged. For the first time in a long time, maybe ever, Sarah said she would miss me. I said I would miss her, and felt it in my bones. I looked over at Tim; even he was a bit emotional, a little misty-eyed. It was a lot: that weekend, that moment. And, after everything, that joy we felt was a privilege, a gift, and we deserved every bit of it.

****

Months later, Sarah and I were talking, or at least texting regularly. I garnered enough courage to share the stories about her I had written for this book. I wanted to make sure she was comfortable with me including them. We set up a Facetime call, with the plan I would read her the stories. She was nervous and so was I. Halfway into the first story, she started to cry. She signaled me to stop reading. She needed a moment to compose herself. Eventually, we got through that story and then the next and the next. By the end, she had taken her glasses off, and she was red-faced, sobbing. I jumped to the conclusion that she was upset with me. That she didn't agree with what I had written. Maybe she even thought I was lying. All I could do was wait for her to be able to speak. It was a torturous few moments.

"Mom," she said. "All this time, I didn't know you were on my side. That you were trying to save me." It was my turn to cry. In relief. In solidarity.

The Grief Competition: My Name Was _____

I suppose I could say that by now, I'm a grief expert. By which I mean to say, I could teach a masterclass, but I do not have all the answers. Maybe I don't have any answers. In this life, I embarked and wandered on my journey with no compass, no directions, no one to ask, and no good place to hide. I just conjured and gutted out the roadmaps to survival as I went along. I figured things out. I was driven to get somewhere better, be someone better.

My mother, and my father, despite their best intentions and hard work, and my grandfather with his sick desires and manipulation, all those terrifying and dark days, were roadside attractions to endure on my life journey. So were the family "friends," the rapists, the boyfriends with their fists and flaws. The teachers, the friends, the women in my family who turned a blind eye, deaf to the howling of my predicaments. Unacknowledging my suffering. But I know this to be true: I outlasted them all.

I'm not entirely sure how I made it, how I survived, how I triumphed. Maybe it's my commitment to my restlessness that kept me tumbling toward safety, something better, toward freedom. I've been ever-moving, seeing rest as a weakness, as a threat. I have been exhausted for so long.

Maybe it's just my sense of invincible optimism that kept me going. I think of my mother, in all her various states of ruin, and wonder how I did not end up like her. My gratitude can remain unspoken. I think of my father, ravaged by alcoholism and bad lungs. I could have gotten both of those genes, but the luck of the draw meant I did not. Every time I drink a glass of wine, and consider having another, I wonder if I'm heading down their bleak road. It's hard not to dwell in that place.

I go back in time, as far as I'm able, as far as I dare. My brain is full of surprises. Recently, at the car dealership, the earthy, smoky, slightly sweet odor of used engine oil made me think of those boys across the street in The Garage, with their black leather jackets, their greasy jeans, and how they made me feel connected to something greater than my very young self. The jars of screws, and the belts and hoses, served as the talismans, lesser gods of the greater car cult. I never remember being afraid, as I stood in The Garage, holding a broom or searching for bottle caps.

Now, when I pop the hood on my little red car, the engine's guts are covered by a breastplate of thick black plastic. It's barely obvious where the dipstick resides, or where to add wiper fluid. I smirk as I lift the hood, as I remember when I was fifteen years old or so, and my father challenged me to find where to put the "blinker fluid." I became the butt of that joke for years, long after I was a proficient and independent driver. Like many memories, that one is sweet with a sting in the tail.

I can't help but wonder how my life would have been different if I had lived as Amy Elizabeth. Maybe my life would have been easier, I would have been tougher, would have been less of an easy victim. Perhaps not, but I feel a deep resentment toward my father for not giving me the opportunity. For being a thief. Even twenty years after his death.

Would Amy Elizabeth have had the gumption to march across the street to The Garage? Would she have survived the abuse, the assaults, the chaos, the fear my life inculcated in me? Sometimes I question how much DNA Amy Elizabeth and I share, though science tells me the answer. But what qualities and traits are mine alone? Would she have dyscalculia? Would numbers spin in front of her, like whirling Dervishes? Nature versus nurture. Discuss.

Trying that name on now makes me feel itchy, like wearing a cedar chest sweater, stinking of mothballs. In adulthood, I know several women named Amy, and while I like them all, none are anything like me.

By another name, I wonder if I would have been a better sister, daughter, or mother. I wonder if I would have been as anguished, as weird as a young girl. Would I have covered the drain in the shower with a washcloth, convinced cameras were watching me, like my grandfather did? Would I have sleepwalked, with no recollection of how I got out on the porch, or in the shower with the water running over my pajamas, wanting to just get clean? Would I have worn double shirts, double pants, and double underwear to my junior high music lessons with the kindest, gentlest French horn teacher named Doug?

But I also wonder if I would have stood side-by-side with my brother, at the Concours D' Elegance at Pebble Beach, or admired the millions of dollars worth of supercars at Monterey Car Week, or ventured to the Talladega Superspeedway, in the pouring rain, that weekend in Alabama? I remember waiting for the track to dry, riding in a race truck, going who-knows how fast, and seeing my brother so happy, anticipating his laps in the red Number 14, Tony Stewart, NASCAR car. Would I have enjoyed the massive Back to The Fifties car shows at the state fairgrounds? Would we have gone to Monaco?

I think about how Tim and I talk about cars. How it's a peculiar connective tissue between us. My brother has an extraordinary knowledge of the makes and models of vehicles. But he is also partially colorblind and has other challenges that are not mine to share here. I pepper him with, "What's that?," and he responds with "What color is that? How about that one?" I can tell a Corvette from a BMW from a Maserati, but he has a seemingly unlimited depth of information on horsepower, features, and Car & Driver reviews. Our father was the same way and had an engineer's skillset without the education. I wish so much that our father had lived longer. That I didn't feel like I let him down in his final years. I wish a lot of things. But wishing is just betting on the past, gambling on an uncertain future.

I haven't cornered the market on grief, and I have no wish

to do so. That is a competition I have no interest in winning. But, what about Amy Elizabeth? Would she have survived this book's immense unburdening? I don't wish it on anyone. I feel both raw and clean. I can almost smell the bleach, as the dark stains of terror, anger, and uncertainty have ebbed away, leaving me exposed and vulnerable, but fully intact.

Perhaps the reality is that Amy Elizabeth has been with me all these decades. Maybe she is the one who drove that tenacious optimism that kept my lights on. I gained and lost one sister in this lifetime; maybe Amy Elizabeth was or is meant to be another. Just maybe. In my eyes-closed imagination, I can see the two of us, Amy Elizabeth and I, in the gold Trans Am with the top down, singing to the radio and driving toward home.

THE END

Acknowledgments

It's hard to even know where to start. First, let me say thank you to Trio House Press. Kris Bigalk, your phone call changed my life. Thank you for your support, your encouragement, and for answering all my emails and endless questions. Special thanks to my editor, Dick Terrill. Your observations, thoughtful suggestions, and ongoing patience helped me see things I never would have. Thank you! We'll both have to start drinking decaf now.

To my writing partner, Mary Kane, for the collaboration, feedback, and your lovely friendship. Thanks, friend.

Thank you to Roy Guzman for your early and ongoing editing and input. Your great ideas helped me think differently and got the ball rolling.

To Diane Wilson, with appreciation. Thank you for telling me to finish the book.

To my early readers with your kind hearts and keen eyes, your questions and your feedback, in no particular order of love or importance: Samson Seiffert, Jenna Seiffert, Marni Ribnick, Tim Gilmore, Tim Thomas, Chris Vanderlinden, Beth Ramsey, Mary Kane, Steven Quade. Thank you!

Much love and thanks to my friends and family who helped me with research, and gently validated (or invalidated) memories and stories. Thanks for helping to wrangle my brain.

To my children, Samson and Sarah, thank you for making me a mom. I couldn't be prouder of you both. Love you.

Deep gratitude to my brother, Tim, for your fact-checking, validation, support, and car knowledge. I treasure our trips together. You're my favorite brother.

And, of course, always and forever my husband, favorite boyfriend, travel buddy, shoulder to cry on, high-fiver, dishwasher-loader, love of my life, Steven. This book would not have happened if it hadn't been for your encouragement and love. Thank you for putting up with me. Kisses.

And finally, Dear Reader, thank you, thank you for reading my words. I hope you, too can find your way.

Previously Published Work

Of Rust and Glass, July 2022, Volume 9, "Colvill Park, 1976"

Pink Panther Magazine, March 2023, Volume 14, Number 1, "A Bible Story"

The Museum of Americana, June 2024, Issue 33, "Sing Your Hymn of the Open Road"

About the Author:

Renee Gilmore is a multi-genre writer, essayist, and poet. She writes about her experiences growing up in a family of car enthusiasts - mechanics, racers, and collectors - and navigating a family full of secrets. She fearlessly explores the illusion of happiness. Through her writing and lived experience, Renee proves that resilience can be practiced both by accident and intention. Renee holds degrees from the University of New Mexico and Hamline University and identifies as a person with a disability. Her work has appeared in many literary journals, including The Louisville Review, Fatal Flaw, and Pink Panther Magazine, among others. She lives in suburban Minneapolis with her husband, Steven, and works in corporate learning and development.

About the Book

Wayfinding: A Memoir was designed at Trio House Press through the collaboration of:

Richard Terrill, Editor
Patrick Werle, Interior Designer
Baonhia Xiong, Cover Designer
Maya Kuvaja, Cover Art

The text is set in Adobe Caslon Pro.

About the Press

Trio House Press is an independent literary press dedicated to discovering, publishing, and promoting books that enhance culture and the human experience. Trio House Press adheres to and supports all ethical standards and guidelines outlined by the CLMP. For further information, or to consider making a donation to Trio House Press, visit us online at triohousepress.org.

www.ingramcontent.com/pod-product-compliance
Lightning Source LLC
Chambersburg PA
CBHW060513080526
44586CB00012B/471